# lost gifts

## Miscarriage, Grief, and the God of All Comfort

"Brittany's book is beautiful, poignant, and—best of all—deeply biblical. Those who have experienced miscarriage will find her a friend, guide, and mentor who offers true hope and lasting comfort even amidst the deepest grief."

—TIM CHALLIES,
author of *Seasons of Sorrow: The Pain of Loss and the Comfort of God*

"Brittany has a gift for offering both gentle friendship and solid truth in all her writing. Her candor about her own story of loss combined with her compassion for others who are hurting offer unique support to all who are walking roads that they wish they weren't."

—MAGGIE COMBS, author of *Motherhood Without All the Rules*

"Women often suffer miscarriage in silence to guard against platitudes and misunderstanding. In *Lost Gifts*, Brittany gives voice to the real and gutting heartache of losing a baby in your womb. She validates a mother's sorrow for her unborn child and guides her to lament freely before the Lord. While Christian cliches may brush off pain, Brittany holds up Scripture as a lifeline. Her honest words invite us to notice God's nearness as we trek through grief. I'm thankful to now have *Lost Gifts* as a resource I can hand to women longing for a Savior who weeps with them."

—JENN HESSE, coauthor of *Waiting In Hope: 31 Reflections for Walking with God Through Infertility*;
content director of Waiting in Hope Ministries

"Miscarriage leaves a scar on our souls, one that—I can attest to—never goes away. Brittany Allen comes alongside the wounded, bleeding heart as she vulnerably shares her journey of suffering and loss through miscarriage and what God has taught her along the way. She does not mince words or slap a bow on the grief of miscarriage; instead, she shows us God's heart of compassion for us, his children. Brittany offers the one thing we need most in our suffering—the comfort of our Savior, who suffered for us and through whom we can grieve with hope."

—GRETCHEN SAFFLES, author of *The Well-Watered Woman: Rooted in Truth, Growing in Grace, Flourishing in Faith*

"*Lost Gifts* will be a balm to the hearts of many who've experienced miscarriage. I've known Brittany for years, and deeply appreciate her care for women who've walked this path of loss. This book helps steward grief and lament in a way that both honors the sorrow, but also points to the steadfast love, sturdy presence, and everlasting hope found in Christ. This book will be a gift to anyone navigating the sorrow of miscarriage."

—CHELSEA SOBOLIK, author of *Longing for Motherhood: Holding On to Hope in the Midst of Childlessness* and *Called to Cultivate: A Gospel Vision for Women and Work*

"It is a lovingkindness to allow people to see your scars so that they might learn compassion. It is a lovingkindness to articulate deep grief so that people might be seen. Brittany Allen has shown us her scars in this book and wrestled with the Scriptures so that we might love God in the midst of suffering."

—EVAN WELCHER, pastor, Grace Baptist Church, Vermillion, South Dakota

"To comfort the suffering with words that are full of truth and grace is nothing short of Christlike, and Brittany has given us this gift in her book. Her honest stories, heartfelt laments, and commitment to God's word will bless anyone who is hurting. I look forward to sharing *Lost Gifts* with grieving moms, as I know they will feel seen, known, and loved through its pages."

—KRISTEN WETHERELL, mom of three (plus two in heaven); author of *Humble Moms: How the Work of Christ Sustains the Work of Motherhood*; coauthor of *Hope When It Hurts: Biblical Reflections to Help You Grasp God's Purpose in Your Suffering*

# lost gifts

## Miscarriage, Grief, and the God of All Comfort

Brittany Lee Allen

*Lost Gifts: Miscarriage, Grief, and the God of All Comfort*



Lexham Press, 1313 Commercial St., Bellingham, WA 98225
LexhamPress.com



Print ISBN 9781683597988
Digital ISBN 9781683597995
Library of Congress Control Number 2024950422

Lexham Editorial: Rachel Joy Welcher, Todd Hains, Erin Mangum, Mandi Newell
Cover Design: Gabriel Eason
Typesetting: Abigail Stocker

25 26 27 28 29 30 31 / US / 12 11 10 9 8 7 6 5 4 3 2 1

To James,
Through your steady love, God has healed many of the broken parts in me. Thank you for choosing me and holding my hand in the fires of this life.

To the babies I never met,
It was my joy to carry you all the days of your life. See you when I get home.

# Contents

# Introduction

*Walk with me behind the house*
*to the place*
*where zinnias grow.*
*It's there where I first sowed*
*seeds of grief—*
*watching and waiting—*
*in the hand-tilled earth.*
*It was when they began to bloom*
*that I first felt death,*
*from within.*

"*There's nothing there,*" I heard myself whisper as tears gathered in my eyes. Contractions pulsed through my abdomen as the tech searched for my baby via internal ultrasound. I shook uncontrollably in a fury of anxiety and sadness as tears slid down my cheek and pooled in my ears. My friend held my hand, repeating the only words to be said at a time like this: "God loves you, Brittany. He loves you so much."

I left the hospital that day with a heart so full of grief, there was no room left for more. But I was forced to make room, as I lost two more precious and deeply loved babies to miscarriage. I felt life perish from within my body three times. Grief upon grief upon grief.

Recurrent pregnancy loss was the diagnosis. Add to that the painful layer of empty arms, and you get a heart that is sick with grief. I wasn't actually experiencing childlessness; I had children. I just never got to hold them or know them or kiss them. And yet, my life looked no different from the outside. Was I barren? I wasn't sure. It felt like barrenness at times. More than that, it felt like death had a grip on my womb—as though the very place meant to nourish a child had become a place where unborn babies went to die.

I write this knowing that I am not the only one who has experienced the heartbreak and confusion of losing a baby in the womb. Women in church pews, down grocery aisles, and sitting in restaurants throughout the world know this pain. One in four pregnancies end in loss. But just because miscarriage is common doesn't make it any less painful. Some women lose one baby. Others experience multiple losses. Many women face both infertility intertwined with miscarriage. And other women lose multiple unborn babies throughout their motherhood journey, between live births. Whether you are blessed with living children or not, the grief of losing any child feels unbearable.

Six years ago, I collapsed into my husband's embrace on the living room floor, writhing in pain while laboring for a lifeless child.

I've witnessed the lives of three babies slip from my body. Grief like this changes a person. Some of you have held the remains of your longed-for baby in your hand. You've seen the image of your empty womb a week after it flickered on the screen with the sight of a strong heartbeat. The lab work, the ultrasounds, the pregnancy announcements, the questions, fears, and emotions—all of them, pointing your mind back to the dreadful refrain: "Your baby is dead." These are the gut-wrenching realities many of us face.

Walking through miscarriage is like a season of storms and steady rain. The storms are like tsunamis, threatening to overtake and drown your life in sorrow. Once the storm is hushed, you're left with unrelenting rain—the steady undertone of sadness as you learn to live without the baby (or babies) you had hoped would be part of your life. What would they have looked like, we wonder? Who would they have become? How would it feel to hold their tiny hand, even just for a moment?

In a culture with so much confusion regarding suffering, we're left with many questions. Is God here? Does he see me? Does he hear me? Most importantly, does he care? As Christian women, we seek biblical answers for how to reconcile the loss of our babies with the mystery of God's sovereignty over our lives. Our feet search for the middle ground between different theological stances. Some declare that if we'd only had enough faith, our babies would have lived. Others believe God has little control over the happenings in life. Well-meaning brothers and sisters sometimes share truths about God's sovereignty, trying to comfort the grieving by telling us that he allowed our children to die for our good—our sanctification—while forgetting to weep alongside us. We find ourselves wrestling with questions. How can God be good and still allow such suffering to enter our lives? Where is God in our pain? Does he care? Yet each question and lament acts as a springboard, catapulting us toward him.

Grief has a way of drawing us to the only one who can truly understand our pain: Jesus, the Man of Sorrows. Our loss reveals our need for God and tosses us hard against him. The absence of our baby can leave us clawing at Jesus's feet at the throne of grace—the place we are promised mercy. If only we could touch him, maybe our heart would be healed.

In losing my three sweet babies, I was not left empty-handed. God filled my hands with his own nail-pierced hands. He met me in my grief and sat with me in the ashes. He will do this for you, too. You can know him—your suffering Savior. To know him more is to treasure him more. Jesus is not a consolation prize for the loss of your unborn babies. He *is* the prize—the Treasure that surpasses all other treasures.

Maybe these truths are hard to believe right now. Maybe you've picked up this book as a last-ditch effort to hold on to your faith in the God who promises to hold his children fast. Whatever your reason for reading, I hope you will walk away encouraged that God is carrying you through this season of grief and that his love for you runs as deep as the sea.

I echo Paul's prayer as my hope for you:

> For this reason I bow my knees before the Father, from whom every family in heaven and on earth is named, that according to the riches of his glory he may grant you to be strengthened with power through his Spirit in your inner being, so that Christ may dwell in your hearts through faith—that you, being rooted and grounded in love, may have strength to comprehend with all the saints what is the breadth and length and height and depth, and to know the love of Christ that surpasses knowledge, that you may be filled with all the fullness of God. (Ephesians 3:14–19)

God loves you. He loves you so much. Let me help you believe it.

## Chapter 1

# The Gift of a Child

## *Lord, Does My Baby's Life Matter?*

*"I also joy, that God hath gain'd one more;*
*To Praise him in the heavens; then was before:*
*And that this babe (as well as all the rest,)*
*since 't had a soule, shalbe for ever blest:"*[1]
—Mary Carey

*Sorrow hangs heavy* in the room. Like an invisible, weighted blanket, sadness presses into her body. She struggles to open her eyes; they're still puffy from last night. Tissues are piled high on her nightstand, telling a story her lips dare not speak. She sits up in bed and her head pounds. It's the Lord's Day. Time to get up—time to pretend everything is okay.

She and her husband slip in the back, hand in hand. They sit in the pew with grief heavy on their hearts, on their marriage, and on their souls. They had decided not to share about the little life in her womb until they reached the twelve-week mark. But twelve weeks never came. Now, they feel silly sharing with others this great loss they've been walking through, and the wounds they've sustained from it. It feels like a burden they must bear alone. What is worse is, she did try to open up to a friend, but she was met with the all too common phrase spoken to women who miscarry: "At least you can get pregnant." That moment sealed the deal. It seemed safer to hide her grief than to be met with words that sting—words that make her feel like her baby isn't valued, or her grief is misplaced.

This is the story of countless women. While some couples share, others feel pressure to keep their baby a secret from all but a select few. "Remember what happened last time," an acquaintance had warned me after my first loss. I quickly lost count of the times I received counsel to hide the wonderful news of new life. Some women choose secrecy to protect their hearts from the questions and comments of friends and family. The fact is most couples who decide to share about their baby as well as their miscarriage are met with responses that hurt and isolate. Maybe a fellow church goer says she had a miscarriage too, but she wasn't nearly as sad. This leaves them feeling like she finds their grief to be unwarranted. Or maybe an older woman brushes off their loss as she says, "It's so common. You'll have another baby."

Women who have experienced miscarriage are met with all kinds of comments, ranging from seriously unhelpful to profoundly hurtful and many times downright unbiblical. Many Christians aren't sure how to respond, so they simply stay silent, ignoring the elephant-sized grief in the room. Couples are expected to move on quickly and are judged when they don't. It often feels that there is little space for the grief of losing a baby in the womb.

In addition to painful comments, women also encounter those within and outside the church who do not value the sanctity of the unborn, causing women who miscarry to ask the question: *Does my baby's life actually matter?* How did pre-born, image-bearers of the Living God become less valuable in the minds of some than those outside of the womb? Why is it that even in Christian circles, so many women feel they must hide their grief? How did we get here?

## Pregnancy and Miscarriage Over the Centuries

Prior to the 1700s, it was widely believed that a child gained a soul when a woman experienced movement in her womb.[2] In these earlier centuries, some who sustained a miscarriage believed they were experiencing what was deemed a false conception. Many believed a miscarriage was the loss of a *potential* child, as we see in this woman's letter to her husband: "The imaginary number 10, whom I had already begun to love, is not a real entity as yet ...".[3] But many did know—long before science could confirm—that they lost more than an "almost" baby. They lost their child who had an eternal soul and was known by God. This quote from a woman written in her diary in 1862 gives a bit of insight into what might have been the experience of many women in previous centuries:

> 15 November. Immediately in the morning I felt severe pains in my belly which became stronger and continued until around 2pm, when I finally gave premature birth to another small child, which seems to have been dead for quite some time. Although I was glad and grateful to be rid of the severe pains and of the aggrieved disposition which I have had for quite some time, this whole episode was difficult for me, and my mind was heavy. Yet I can also thank the Saviour and trust in him that it is the best for me.[4]

Here we see evidence of grief in a woman whose "mind was heavy" after the loss of her unborn baby. She calls the tiny baby a child, acknowledging what has always been true about life in a mother's womb. Unfortunately, not all women during that time would have agreed with her. It's easy to look back on previous centuries and imagine them to have naturally upheld the sanctity of life better than we do in our time. But all generations are filled with people who constantly repeat old patterns of previous sinners. Perhaps if they'd known more, they might have upheld those tiny lives better than we do today. The truth is, for many years humans were left to guess about the happenings in the womb. Even some Christians weren't sure when conception truly took place. It was believed for a long time that a baby in the womb was just a clump of cells. Those who advocated for abortion rights harped on this very point. That was, until science caught up with reality.

### *Scientific Advancement and Greater Understanding of Life in the Womb*

We are blessed with major scientific advancement in our time regarding pregnancy. Until recent centuries, the process of how new life came into the world was mostly a mystery. No one fully understood how a human was conceived, only that it happened sometime after a man and woman had sex. This led to many false theories in the eighteenth and nineteenth centuries. As *New York Times* contributor Abraham Verghese explains in his article *Where Do Babies Come from? And Why Did It Take Scientists so Long to Find Out?,* in the 1800s, many believed that a single sperm held an entire human being, while others thought the preformed human was in the maternal egg. He also shares that it wasn't until the year 1876 that the process of fertilization was discovered.[5]

While you and I can reach under our bathroom sink to grab a pregnancy test, the first somewhat reliable test to detect HCG (the pregnancy hormone) was only available through a doctor in 1970. At-home tests came on the market as recently as 1978.[6] This means, until very recent years, women had to rely on signs in their own body, from the missing period to the onset of nausea to determine if they were pregnant. It must have been very confusing for women who experienced miscarriage in the early weeks of pregnancy. Did they lose a baby? Or was their period late?

It's not uncommon for a woman to begin to miscarry when she was expecting her period. Maybe this is part of your story. Many of these women feel like something isn't quite right, so they take a test only to discover their suspicion was valid—they had conceived a baby. Many of us feel the evidence of our baby before we ever see the two lines that prove it. Yet often, when a woman miscarries, she's met with assumptions about women in the past: "It was easier back then. Women didn't know they were pregnant because they didn't have early pregnancy tests like we do today." It's believed that not having a confirmed pregnancy saved women a lot of grief. But is it really logical that the majority of women who fell pregnant and then miscarried shortly after were so aloof to the happenings of their body? Is it really better that they hadn't known for sure—to be left always wondering? Many of us have felt the change within our bodies prior to confirming with a test. Though women in earlier times didn't have the access to testing we have today, we shouldn't be too quick to assume that they must not have known they were pregnant and therefore didn't grieve as deeply.

Technology continued to advance, as science finally caught up with what we all know is true: life begins at conception. While mothers today can listen to their baby's heartbeat as early as 10 weeks gestation, this wasn't possible until a fetal doppler monitor was created in 1964. We learned even more through ultrasound technology, a phenomenon that was only available in hospitals as recently as the late 1970s. In fact, my mother, who gave birth to both of her children in the late 80s, never had an ultrasound during her pregnancies. The invention of the ultrasound has given us incredible insight into the womb and into a baby's development from conception to birth. Many of us have heard our baby's heartbeat or witnessed their wiggling on the screen. When my husband and I saw our first baby on a fuzzy black screen at only 7 weeks pregnant, our eyes were glued to the tiny flicker before us. There was no question about it—we were beholding *life.* While fetal doppler monitors detect a heartbeat as early as 8–10 weeks gestation, the ultrasound allows us to capture the heartbeat of a pre-born child as early as *five weeks*: a heartbeat that thumps with the truth of life; its rhythm, an anthem of praise to the Creator.

Nearly all biologists, including those who consider themselves to be pro-choice, now agree life begins at conception. A study found on PubMed states, "Biologists from 1,058 academic institutions around the world assessed survey items on when a human's life begins and, overall, 96% (5337 out of 5577) affirmed the fertilization view."[7] The evidence of what you and I know in our hearts and have felt in our bodies is undeniable.

### *The Popularization of Abortion*

Tragically, abortion law advocacy rapidly rose in the 1960s and was later legalized in 1973. All of this happened before ultrasounds became a routine part of pregnancy. Even after all of the medical, scientific, and technological advancement over the centuries, the value of babies in the womb is still under attack.

The very existence of abortion is utterly painful for the woman walking through miscarriage. We see the signs and hear the words that seek to diminish the lives of our unborn children, and we mourn. We get angry. And rightly so. We live in a day and age where babies are no longer viewed as gifts from above but are instead treated as hindrances to our dreams. We read stories and headlines like when actress Michelle Williams said, as she held a baby in her belly and a Golden Globe in her fist, "I wouldn't have been able to do this without employing a woman's right to choose."[8] We grieve. We wonder why she gets to keep her baby when ours has passed away. And yet, she is following the ways of this world. We are the women who've grown up being fed the lie that the vulnerable babies within our wombs are dispensable—just a tiny clump of cells without personhood and without worth. Our mothers were taught this lie, and our grandmothers weren't really sure what to believe, let alone the generations prior to that. Of course this has an impact on how our society, and sadly a portion of the church, views children in the womb.

Most abortion advocates admit that a pre-born baby is human. They just don't believe that the baby has gained personhood yet. This is called personhood theory. It's the theory that the body is separate from the mind; it claims you can be human without being a person. The French philosopher René Descartes coined what is referred to as two-story dualism in the seventeenth century. Some think this is where personhood theory finds its roots.[9] In her book, *Love Thy Body*, Nancy R. Pearcey does an incredible job at tackling this difficult but necessary topic for our time:

> Virtually no professional bioethicist denies that life begins at conception. In the two-story metaphor, however, to talk about the fetus as biologically human is in the lower Story,

> the realm of Science—where the body has been reduced to a mindless machine to be used and exploited, like the rest of nature. It is just a disposable piece of matter. This explains why being biologically human is no longer thought to confer any moral status or to warrant legal protection. To be human is no longer equivalent to being a person. Human life has been reduced to raw material with no intrinsic purpose or dignity, subject to whatever purposes we choose to impose.[10]

Our society has taken what God has created as good—pre-born children—and called them a burden; his image-bearers have been deemed expendable. Sadly, the church is not immune to wrong thinking about life in the womb. After losing our third baby to miscarriage, a well-meaning friend compared me to a mutual friend who had been struggling with infertility for years. "Think about her. How terrible. At least you can get pregnant." The breath in my lungs was stolen for a moment as pain gripped my heart. When a woman receives comments about her miscarriage like "Is it even a baby yet?" "At least it was early," "You'll have another baby," "At least you have other children," or "It's so common," what she hears is: "Your baby doesn't matter. Your baby wasn't a real life. Your baby isn't worth grieving." In a poll on social media, I asked women who have miscarried if they felt they had to hide their grief from others. Forty-eight percent of those who replied said "Yes." Maybe you have felt the same.

### *A Culture of Silence*

Another common response to miscarriage from older generations is to claim: "In our days of child-rearing, we didn't talk about miscarriage." They seem to mean that women shouldn't talk about their loss because miscarriage is something to be endured privately. This may have been due to the confusion about what a miscarriage truly was or because of the growing popularity of abortion. Likewise, the common occurrence of miscarriage led many to wrongly view such loss as simply part of the journey of motherhood. This could be the reason we mainly hear "Miscarriage is so common," from the lips of older women. They're right; it is common, but that doesn't make it less painful. That doesn't make it okay. And it in no way changes the value of the baby who was lost.

It's hard to pinpoint the origins of the popular 12-week rule, which is the unwritten rule that a woman should keep her pregnancy a secret until she reaches twelve weeks gestation, when the likelihood of miscarriage significantly drops. Doctors, family members, and friends encourage women to withhold from sharing just in case she miscarries. Many of us follow this cultural rule as we walk through the most vulnerable weeks in pregnancy (from fear of loss to unbearable sickness) with very little support. When tragedy strikes—when a heartbeat goes silent or a D&C is needed—many women and couples feel they must grieve their baby without much support as well.

Some of the women I've conversed with over the years have said they wanted to grieve privately, explaining further that it was because they didn't want to face hurtful comments. This is understandable; it is also heartbreaking. The church has fallen prey to wrong views about the unborn and spoken words that have diminished their lives, wounding our brothers and sisters (more on this in chapter nine). We've developed a church culture which leaves many couples to suffer in the very silence we've cultivated. I hope that one day as believers we will change our language surrounding life in the womb to match our Creator's. In doing so, women like you and me might feel freer to grieve our baby openly.

Misunderstanding the whole process of procreation over the years has influenced our culture and the way we all think about life now. The comments that question the life and value of our babies when we miscarry can be traced back to our culture and to our past. This doesn't make the comments any less painful, but it can be helpful to see why we are so often met with poor counsel and thoughtless words when we experience miscarriage.

Our culture longs for us to swim in its current. Those who oppose life want us to keep quiet about babies in the womb. Yet every baby, whether the size of a poppyseed or a watermelon, is worthy of our rejoicing; and they are worthy of our grieving when they pass away. No matter what our society says, our babies are image-bearers of the Living God. They have immense value.

## Bearing the Image of the Living God

So, what gives a person value? Is it our gender, our heritage, our net worth? Some might say we are valuable based on what we can offer the world around us or our intelligence level. Is our value based on whether we are wanted by our parents? Age, background, looks, skin color, talent—there are a host of things people use to evaluate someone's worth.

We've spent a good chunk of time talking about how our past has influenced our thinking about life in the womb. To discover the answer to our original question (do our babies' lives matter?), we need to go back to the very beginning. We need to go back to the Source of all living things.

The Bible begins with God's creation of all things in heaven and on earth. He creates stars, planets, galaxies, flowers, animals, and insects. His word goes forth, and the ocean is formed—vast and deep, midnight blue and turquoise. Grains of sand rest on the shore, and mountains with their peaks in the sky appear across the world. It's beautiful and it's good.

The most cherished part of his creation, though, are the people, both male and female, whom he creates in his own image (Genesis 1:27). Each and every person's value is found here; all people have the same beginning—being crafted in the hands of a mighty God. We are made in his likeness (Genesis 5:1; James 3:9). Every one of us, aside from the very first humans, Adam and Eve, were created in the shadow of a mother's womb.

> For you formed my inward parts;
>     you knitted me together in my mother's womb.
> I praise you, for I am fearfully and wonderfully made.
> Wonderful are your works;
>     my soul knows it very well.

> My frame was not hidden from you,
> when I was being made in secret,
> intricately woven in the depths of the earth.
> Your eyes saw my unformed substance;
> in your book were written, every one of them,
> the days that were formed for me,
> when as yet there was none of them. (Psalm 139:13–16)

While a baby in the womb may be hidden from the eyes of human beings, nothing is kept secret from God. In fact, he is the one who carefully knits each of us together cell by cell. Psalm 139 doesn't only speak to our humanness, but also to our *personhood*. We were known by our Creator even when we were an unformed ovum, zygote, embryo, or fetus. Even before our lungs were shaped or our heart began to beat, God had numbered each of our days. We are "fearfully and wonderfully made" and this points us to the God whose works are wonderful. Every person—every single baby in the womb—is not only made by a holy God, but also crafted in his own image, and, therefore has intrinsic value that can never be stripped away (Genesis 9:6). Though the world may try to devalue the precious lives of preborn children, the truth of the *imago Dei* stands firm.

## The Gift of Your Baby

Your baby is invaluable. Their life—no matter how short—matters. God created each individual to bear his image and bring him glory. Every child is a blessing. This includes the ones we never got to meet on earth. They are gifts from above, even if we only knew of their existence for a few days.

The problem with the term "pregnancy loss" is that it's dishonest about the gravity of what was lost. We didn't only lose a pregnancy. We didn't just lose a potential child. It wasn't a false conception. No, when we experience miscarriage, we are grieving the loss of a baby who lived, a baby with an eternal soul. We're grieving our son or daughter whom we already loved. We may have imagined what it would be like to meet them, to see their first smile, or to hold their little hand. To comfort them in sickness and rejoice over their growth. They are our children and we are their mothers. Nothing can change that truth.

Some of you have never experienced a live birth and your home echoes of silence in the very places you hoped to hear the rambunctious giggles of a child. My heart aches for you. I remember. I can easily recall the vacant nursery, the unused onesie, the sight of a round belly, the passing due dates, and the emptiness of Mother's Day. You feel like a mother; your arms ache to hold your baby or babies. You've received the gift of a child but didn't get to live out your motherhood further than the womb. Hear me when I say, *you are a mother*. Your baby—this beautiful gift given to you to steward for a short time—is held by God in heaven. One day, Jesus Christ, our Savior, will rescue us from this world and take us to be with him in heaven where our sweet babies are (2 Samuel 12:23). I don't know what that will look like, but I know we will celebrate and we will finally meet them. We will *know* them.

We can celebrate their lives now, too, even as we grieve. We are free to weep deeply over losing them and missing them while also remembering the gift it is to have carried them in our womb for all their days on earth. Let us praise God for creating them and for bringing them safely to glory, until with bated breath we finally set our eyes on their faces.

Views about life and personhood in the culture and past centuries have indeed influenced the way many people speak of babies in the womb. I hope in this book you will find freedom to grieve your child. Your baby is real. Your baby is a person with a soul. Your baby's life is *invaluable*. You are meant to lament when they die. Your grief is valid.

*At the end of each chapter, you will find a prayer of lament from the Bible. I have also provided space for you to write your own. Below is an example of how to do this:

## Psalm of Lament

My soul is bereft of peace;
I have forgotten what happiness is;
so I say, "My endurance has perished;
so has my hope from the LORD."

Remember my affliction and my wanderings,
the wormwood and the gall!
My soul continually remembers it
and is bowed down within me.
But this I call to mind,
and therefore I have hope:

The steadfast love of the LORD never ceases;
his mercies never come to an end;
they are new every morning;
great is your faithfulness.
"The LORD is my portion," says my soul,
"therefore I will hope in him."
The LORD is good to those who wait for him,
to the soul who seeks him.
It is good that one should wait quietly
for the salvation of the LORD. (Lamentations 3:17–26)

## Guided Lament

God, I have no peace about the loss of my baby. I don't even remember how to be happy; I have no strength left even to hope in you. Remember me, God. Remember how I writhed in pain on the floor, laboring my baby. God, I wanted my baby so much. My soul remembers constantly—it won't let me forget. Help me to hope in you again. You are faithful to me. Prove your goodness to me in this, Lord. Help me believe it. For Jesus's sake Amen.

## Bring Your Lament to God:

## Chapter 2

# The Gift of Lament

## *Lord, Why Did You Take Our Baby?*

*You were carried in my body*
*for nine weeks.*
*Until,*
*I held your small frame in my hands*
*and wept.*
*A flood of salt-water tears.*
*"You have kept count of my tossings;*
*put my tears in your bottle."*[11]
*I wonder, did God ask the angels for more bottles?*

*Tear stains on the delicate pages* of my Bible mark one of my lowest points throughout our miscarriages. After losing three babies back-to-back-to-back within a year, my crushed heart just couldn't bear up under the weightiness of the negative pregnancy test I held in my hands. It was the time where I was most deeply grieved, feeling nearly forsaken by God. With desperation I cried out to him for comfort, for a reprieve from grief.

*"How long, O Lord?"*

David's prayer of lament sprung from my lips (Psalm 13:1). An avalanche of tears followed until words could no longer be spoken with clarity. I took comfort in the fact that the Spirit was interceding the groans of my heart (Romans 8:26). Groans like, *"Lord, why do you keep taking our babies?"*

Recurrent miscarriage had led me to the depths, echoing heartfelt prayers of previous suffering saints. Miscarriage can cause a woman to "drench her couch with her weeping" as I did that day (Psalm 6:6). Surely, "my eyes wasted away because of grief" (Psalm 6:7). God is the giver of all good gifts, but it began to feel like all God did was *take* from me. If you've felt that way too, you're not alone.

This was a turning point for me, though I didn't know it at the time. When I look back, I recognize it as the moment I began to understand a key truth: lament is a necessary part of the Christian walk. Though I'm a deep feeler and an easy crier, I had to open my heart up to lament. Heavy burdens had been placed on my back under the banner of "suffering well," which left little to no room for a heart burdened with sadness. My husband and I walked through our losses in an environment that seemed to view sorrow as evidence of faithlessness and self-pity. Being downcast was often spoken of as if it were sinful. Yet, Scripture never makes that case. My honest prayers of lament were smothered by an unbiblical model of what it looks like to suffer as a disciple of Jesus. I had to learn the dirge of lament. I had to learn that it was okay to go to God with my deepest groans. The three sweet babies who slipped through my fingers and out of my womb were my guides, each leading me one step further in my journey of lament and ultimately closer to God.

## What is Biblical Lament?

Simply put, biblical lament is the act of crying out to God in our sorrow. We bring him everything that's broken in us—our body, our heart, our mind—and we lay it bare before the only one who can heal us. The only one who can truly envelop us with a blanket of comfort. Biblical lament is leading us somewhere. Rather than just complaining to complain, it's the act of crying out to our loving Father for help. Lament leads the believer into deeper communion with God. Lament is *worship*.

Scripture is not silent on this topic. There are many examples showing us we are free to approach God with tear-streaked cheeks and pain in our hearts. There's a whole book titled *Lamentations*. Job calls out to the Lord in his compounded grief after losing his children, servants, livelihood, and finally his health. Hannah, who suffered years of infertility, "was deeply distressed and prayed to the LORD and wept bitterly." She was so inconsolable that Eli, the priest, mistook her to be drunk (1 Samuel 1:10–14). We, like Hannah, can pour out our soul before the Lord (1 Samuel 1:15). These stories of fellow sufferers are a balm to women walking through the grief of losing a baby in the womb.

Here are just a few passages among many examples of lament in the Bible. Take care to read them. They may be the very echo of your own soul.

As we face miscarriage …

Grief wears on our soul:

> I am weary with my moaning,
> every night I flood my bed with tears;
> I drench my couch with my weeping.
> My eye wastes away because of grief;
> it grows weak because of all my foes. (Psalm 6:6–7)

We might feel forgotten or forsaken:

> How long, O Lord? Will you forget me forever?
> How long will you hide your face from me?
> How long must I take counsel in my soul
> and have sorrow in my heart all the day? (Psalm 13:1–2a)

We feel weary to our bones:

> Be gracious to me, O Lord, for I am in distress;
> my eye is wasted from grief;
> my soul and my body also.
> For my life is spent with sorrow,
> and my years with sighing;
> my strength fails because of my iniquity,
> and my bones waste away. (Psalm 31:9–10)

We long for our baby and sigh from the gripping pain in our heart; we feel abandoned by others:

> I am feeble and crushed;
> I groan because of the tumult of my heart.
>
> O Lord, all my longing is before you;
> my sighing is not hidden from you.
> My heart throbs; my strength fails me,
> and the light of my eyes—it also has gone from me.
> My friends and companions stand aloof from my plague,
> and my nearest kin stand far off. (Psalm 38:8–11)

We cry out to God:

> I am weary with my crying out;
> my throat is parched.
> My eyes grow dim
> with waiting for my God. (Psalm 69:3)

We experience times of deep sorrow, downcastness, or even depression:

> My soul is bereft of peace;
> I have forgotten what happiness is;
> so I say, "My endurance has perished;
> so has my hope from the LORD."
>
> Remember my affliction and my wanderings,
> the wormwood and the gall!
> My soul continually remembers it
> and is bowed down within me. (Lamentations 3:17–20)

Where are you, Lord? Have you forgotten me? When will you intervene? Why are you sleeping? Why do you hide your face from me? These gut-wrenching questions and accusations written down for us by the Holy Spirit in God's holy word are proof that we can—and *should*—bring all of our wrestlings, questions, and emotions to God. We don't need to hide our grief, anger, or confusion from him—we can't. He knows every word on our tongue before we speak it (Psalm 139:4).

In many of the psalms of lament (though not all of them), we watch as the writer moves from prayer to praise somewhat quickly. A lot of Christians point out that though these particular psalms start with a psalmist in torment, he turns around in the end and rejoices in God. Many want to hurry past the "Will you forget me forever?" and jump straight to the "I will sing to the Lord, because he has dealt bountifully with me" (Psalm 13:6). We'd rather skip through the grief and camp out in the praise and thanksgiving. That's a natural response. None of us want to hurt, nor do we like to see others suffer. But grief and lament aren't tidy. The steps we take toward God while in distress certainly won't be marked by perfection. Instead, they're full of stumbling and struggling and fighting to keep going.

Lament is perseverance in faithfulness: A faith held up and sustained by Christ amidst devastation. When everything falls apart, lament is a holy pursuit of our holy God. It's how we worship from the depths.

Why would we run to God with our sorrowful and desperate prayers over our baby? Because we know he is good and sovereign. He is the source of true comfort (2 Corinthians 1:3–5). Biblical lament is an act of worship because it echoes these truths to the world around us and to our own hearts. In his book, *Dark Clouds, Deep Mercy*, Mark Vroegop describes lament as "a prayer in pain that leads to trust." He goes on to explain this further and makes an important point:

> Lament is a path to praise as we are led through our brokenness and disappointment. The space between brokenness and God's mercy is where the song is sung. Think of lament as the transition between pain and promise. It is the path from heartbreak to hope.[12]

Lament is how we turn to God in prayer when faced with the sorrow of miscarriage. If we don't know how to do this or aren't willing to open our hearts to God in this way, we miss out on the joy of communion with him and experiencing his comfort. We cannot escape suffering in this world. We are promised it will come for each of us. Lament helps us know where to go when the heartbeat can't be found, when the pregnancy symptoms vanish, or when one miscarriage turns into two, then three, and then four. It reminds us that when it seems like no one understands or cares about the babies we've lost, God, our Father, *does*.

For some of us, lamenting may come naturally. For others, it's harder. For the more difficult times, it might be helpful to think through what keeps us from lamenting.

## Roadblocks to Lament

Lament can be hard because it is inherently intimate. It can make us feel exposed to lament our baby. Cultural lies about unborn babies can feed into that feeling. Some believe a miscarriage should be grieved privately rather than openly. When the culture and even fellow Christians call for silence regarding early life in the womb, it can make us wonder if the vulnerability of lamenting our baby should be kept to ourselves. Vulnerability is highly uncomfortable for most people. Yet, since God knows us better than we know ourselves, we need not fear being vulnerable with our Creator. Our loving Father longs for us to draw near to him when we are hurting. Just as a child runs to their mom or dad with a scraped knee, we can run to him with the grief of our baby heavy on our heart.

Lament can also leave us vulnerable in a different way. The unfortunate truth is, other believers may judge us harshly for our tears over our baby. They may misunderstand us in our grief, which is a deeply isolating experience. Maybe they even begin to think that our strong emotions over the loss of our baby are a sign of weak faith and immaturity. The hurt this causes can feel massively cruel as we nurse the open wounds left by our miscarriage. We must fight to not allow this to prevent us from bringing our honest prayers before the God of all comfort.

Furthermore, many of us don't know how to lament because we've never been taught. Our church culture (particularly in the United States, from which I write) has taught us that happiness is required at all times to be a faithful Christian. This way of thinking leads many to conceal their sorrow under statements like "God is good!" We confuse verses in the Bible that remind us to "rejoice always" with "don't ever be sad." Lament gives us permission to be deeply grieved over our child *and* genuinely joyful over God's unchanging goodness at the same time. It's possible to cry out to God in sorrow and rejoice in our salvation in the very same breath. These emotions aren't mutually exclusive. Some Christians view grief in a way that leans more closely to modern-day stoicism than a biblical view of suffering. They act like the Stoics in John Calvin's day:

> At present, likewise, there are among Christians new Stoics who think it a vice not only to groan and weep but even to be sad or upset ... But this cruel philosophy is nothing to us. Our Master and Lord condemned it not only by word but also by example. Our Lord groaned and wept, both for His own and others' difficult circumstances ... And, so that no one should turn such weeping and lamenting into sin, He expressly declared those who mourn to be blessed.[13]

I've come across Christians who look at any sign of discouragement, sadness, or grief as if it is sinful—as if to be downcast is a sin rather than a part of being a human living in a sin-soaked world. But grieving what God grieves is a sign of ordered emotions and mature faith. Our grief over our baby is evidence that we have loved, and to love is a strength which points to the God who created us, who is love (1 John 4:7–8). Kelly M. Kapic puts it this way:

> Nevertheless, any who have truly lived and loved must come to believe that lament is at least part of our existence. Only the idealistic and unloving belittle tears and sadness. Only the coolly detached never raise a complaint about the condition of things, including our broken bodies. If we never lament, then it is legitimate to wonder if we have ever truly loved.[14]

If we always avoid lament, pretend like we're unaffected by sorrow, and refuse to go to God in our suffering, we reveal a sense of self-sufficiency in our hearts. But we need God; we need the practice of lament to do its work in our hearts. I love this quote by Esther Fleece: "Spiritual maturity does not mean living a lamentless life; rather, it means we grow into becoming good lamenters and thus grow in our need for God."[15] Losing a baby in the womb rightly causes us to cry out to God in lament, and lament puts our need on display. We have always been needy. Growing in recognition of our need for the Lord forces us to put off self-sufficiency and put on the Lord Jesus Christ.

## You Are Free to Lament

If you picked up this book, chances are you are hurting over the loss of your sweet, precious baby. Some of you may be grieving the loss of multiple unborn children—grief upon grief upon grief. You might be experiencing trauma from a D&C or labor pains that happened too soon, ER visits or unsympathetic doctors, the sights, the smells, and the memories. You might be confused because you weren't planning to be pregnant. The baby in your womb changed the trajectory of your life; it seems like your life was interrupted with a gift you didn't know you wanted and then that gift was swiped from your hands. Some of you watch as only one line forms on another pregnancy test, bringing old grief to the surface. You feel a sense of childlessness as you move about your home that's empty of baby gear and giggles. Yet, you *are* a mother. You just never got to hold or kiss or know your baby. The grief of that presses heavily on your heart. There are some of you who have other children and find yourself bearing the burden of their loss too. They ask, "why did my baby brother die?" and you hide in the bathroom as you weep for a world free of sin's curse.

Whether you're fresh on the heels of loss or it happened months or even years ago, God has given you the freedom to run to him with your sorrow. You can boldly approach his throne of grace and find help in your time of need (Hebrews 4:16). He will not chastise you for your pain. He will only listen and draw near to you in your broken-heartedness (Psalm 34:18).

## The God Who Hears and Weeps

When the Israelites were held in captivity by the Egyptians, they cried out to God for deliverance, lamenting their oppression. God saw their affliction, heard their cry, knew their suffering, and finally "came down to deliver them out of the hand of the Egyptians" (Exodus 3:7–8). Yet, this was after many years of suffering and slavery. We can imagine they might have felt like their prayers were bouncing off the stars. But God had been working toward their deliverance long before their lament left their lips. We see evidence when infant Moses was put into a basket to travel safely in the Nile River until he was rescued by Pharaoh's daughter. This was the very same baby that God would one day use to free his people.

Some of you are in a season of ongoing loss. You are weary. You wonder if God really does hear. If he cares, why isn't he rescuing you from this pain? God is constantly orchestrating all things for the good of his people, even when we can't see it. The God who created you knows your sorrow; he knows every thought that passes from your heart to your mind. He knows when you're confused, angry, and cast down. He knows when you're struggling to trust him. He understands your frame and that sometimes it's hard to believe he's good when faced with the death of your baby. God sees, he knows, and he *cares*. More than that, he *acts*. He leans in to listen to your lament and bends down to weep with you (Psalm 40:1; John 11:35).

At one point during Jesus's ministry on earth, he was told that his friend Lazarus was ill. Instead of rushing to save him he said, "This illness does not lead to death. It is for the glory of God, so that the Son of God may be glorified through it" (John 11:4). Not long after, Lazarus breathed his last breath. It must have looked like they had believed in the wrong guy. But Jesus's comment is hinting at something. Jesus knew what would unfold over the next 72 hours. He knew that after four days in the tomb, he would bring the breath of life back into Lazarus's lifeless body. But before Jesus raised Lazarus from the grave, he paused. He knelt down and wept with his loved ones. He wept over their loss as well as his own. He knew within moments he would call Lazarus back to life, and still, he *wept* over him.

Jesus knows all that we cannot see—that he will turn the sorrow we feel for our ultimate good. God knows that in the end all will be made right. He will wipe away every tear and death will die. He's the God of the resurrection. Yet he doesn't hurry us along in our grieving; he doesn't leave us to suffer alone in the now.

I know what it's like to endure grief and feel like God is silent. But he's there in the hurt and grief and confusion—in these days, hours, minutes, where life feels heavy and hard. He's present when babies we longed for so deeply never take a breath or when our arms ache as we watch our friends cradle their own babies. He cares about how our breath is stolen when we see a child the same age that our baby would have been—a stark reminder of all that we've missed. A dagger straight through the heart. In all of this, he weeps with us and grieves our babies alongside us. We are free to lament to the God who weeps with those who weep. Not just free, but encouraged to do so.

## Run to God

Biblical lament is a gift given to us by our good and gracious Father. Mark Vroegop reminds us that "Christianity suffers when lament is missing."[16] The very act of running to God with our tears and questions is healing. It helps us fix our eyes on Jesus, grows our trust in him, reminds us of his promises and faithfulness, humbles us before him, and restores our faith. I know it can be hard. But the habit of running to God in your grief will only deepen your faith in him. If you can't find words or the strength to say them, the Holy Spirit will intercede. God knows every emotion you feel. Sit before him in silent pain or cry out to him in desperation. Lament can look different from person to person or even from one hour to the next. God is waiting and willing to listen to your prayers of lament. No longer do we have to hide behind platitudes. We are free to pour out our soul to God.

If you aren't sure where to start, I recommend journaling your cares to God and then reading them to him. On a particularly difficult day I journaled:

> My heart is filled with such sorrow today. It creeps up on me just when I think I'm okay. I remember what it felt like to feel the evidence of life growing in my womb. As I sit here, *It Is Well* just came on. "When sorrows like sea billows roll, whatever my lot thou hast taught me to say it is well with my soul." It is well, Lord. It just hurts. I need your comfort.

You can pray his word back to him using psalms of lament as your guide. There are many songs for suffering saints that you can listen to and sing to the Lord, even through tears. Your tears are precious to him: "You have kept count of my tossings; put my tears in your bottle. Are they not in your book?" (Psalm 56:8).

Learning how to lament is an ongoing journey in my life. It has been one of God's greatest gifts to me to learn I can run to him in my grief. I pray that today you will see the value of running to him in your grief as well. I pray that you will feel the freedom to lament your baby. I hope you will take it for the gift it is.

## Psalm of Lament

How long, O Lord? Will you forget me forever?
How long will you hide your face from me?
How long must I take counsel in my soul
and have sorrow in my heart all the day?
How long shall my enemy be exalted over me?

Consider and answer me, O Lord my God;
light up my eyes, lest I sleep the sleep of death,
lest my enemy say, "I have prevailed over him,"
lest my foes rejoice because I am shaken.

But I have trusted in your steadfast love;
my heart shall rejoice in your salvation.
I will sing to the Lord,
because he has dealt bountifully with me. (Psalm 13)

## Guided Lament

How long, Lord? When will you bring a reprieve from grief? It feels like you've forsaken me. Please show me I'm wrong. Amen.

## Bring Your Lament to God:

## Chapter 3

# The Gift of a Deepened Theology of Suffering

## *Lord, Is the Death of My Baby Good?*

*The secret things belong to the Lord.*
*Secret things;*
*When labor rushes in too soon.*
*Secret things;*
*Why my babies keep dying.*
*Secret things;*
*The exact moment a heart stops beating, living.*
*Secret things;*
*How long, O Lord?*
*Man should not guess at*
*Secret things.*

*Our nursery became* a storage room. Ultrasound pictures and white tests with twin pink lines were tucked away as keepsakes. The grief of it all was a steady rain, a storm that wouldn't end. I had carried three babies within my body over the course of a year but hadn't been able to hold a single one. My womb remained empty, and I could feel that people didn't know what to do with me anymore. Or what to say. I sensed their weariness over hearing about our grief. Shouldn't I be over it by now?

There were a few close friends who stuck by my side through the joys and sorrows of our pregnancies. They loved me well. Yet, there were some to whom my grief seemed a plague—something to be rid of. Some who claimed to love us stayed silent and it echoed into the distance between us as we lost more babies. Some had particular ideas about how one should grieve miscarriages and I was not passing the test. Unfounded accusations flew, motives were assumed, thoughtless words were spoken, and my tears were judged.

Have you ever experienced condemnation when you needed prayer? Rather than the mercy your tears deserved, you were crushed under hurtful words. Sorrow met with silence. Tears, with judging eyes. I believe a lot of these responses stem from a larger issue in the Western Church—an unbiblical theology of suffering.

There are a variety of harmful teachings about suffering within Christian culture (i.e., prosperity gospel, Word of Faith movement, New Apostolic Reformation, etc.). It would take a whole book to tackle them. But there is an increasingly common response to grief, in which the harm may not be so obvious. One woman calls it "prosperity gospel backwash," which is a fitting name.[17] It's a theology of suffering built around an unbiblical view of what it means to suffer well.

## Emotional Prosperity

While prosperity gospel proponents claim we can control the hand of God by having enough faith, there's a sneakier prosperity teaching creeping into many churches. Here's what it says: if we truly love Jesus more than anything, we won't be phased by woes of the world. We will be so joyful in Christ that heartbreak over things like babies dying in the womb won't deeply grieve us. Basically, prosperity teaching—but make it *emotional*. Rather than gaining earthly blessings by how much faith we have, this ideology teaches that our happiness is determined by how much love for God we have when we are in the grip of suffering things like miscarriage. It operates from an underlying belief that any sort of sadness or discouragement is a sign of weak faith. Some would even say these emotions are sinful. In fact, in these contexts, mental health struggles like anxiety or depression are often deemed a sin problem. Rather than encouraging vulnerability, tears are viewed as indications of immature faith.

Prosperity gospel teachers cry out, "If you had more faith, your baby would have lived." Emotional prosperity teachers say, "If you treasured God above all, you wouldn't be this sad about the loss of your baby." It can begin to feel that the believer's very love for God is brought under scrutiny when they face loss.

These Christians know and recognize that suffering is inevitable. They just believe a mature Christian, who really loves the Lord, won't be greatly affected by the trials of this life. There is little room for feelings of sadness, sorrow, or grief in this way of thinking. If the sufferer feels too deeply for too long, there must be something wrong with their faith. Maybe they're idolizing their baby over God. Maybe they lack spiritual maturity or wisdom. Or worse, some may even question the genuineness of the sufferer's salvation.

This incorrect view of suffering is easy to miss. Often it is only by experiencing the pain it causes and feeling the millstones it places around your neck that you begin to see how damaging it is.

## Suffering Well

Sitting in church, I listened to the pastor make his case. His thesis was: when we are downcast, we reveal we aren't suffering well, and this leads unbelievers away from the gospel. "Why would they want to become Christians when so many of them look like they're so downcast all the time?" he asked. He believed it is our joy in Christ that draws people to the Lord. And I do believe that is the case sometimes, but not all the time. Maybe not even most of the time. The Bible claims it is our *love* for one another that shows Jesus to the world (John 13:35). Loving others sometimes leads us to rejoicing and other times leads us to weeping.

In Peter's first letter, he encourages his audience to honor the Lord and defend the reason for their hope in Christ, but to do so with gentleness and respect. "For it is better to suffer for doing good, if that should be God's will, than for doing evil" (1 Peter 3:14–17). This is the first look into what it means to suffer well. It is to suffer for doing the right thing. Later in the epistle, we find this key passage:

> Beloved, do not be surprised at the fiery trial when it comes upon you to test you, as though something strange were happening to you. But rejoice insofar as you share Christ's sufferings, that you may also rejoice and be glad when his glory is revealed. If you are insulted for the name of Christ, you are blessed, because the Spirit of glory and of God rests upon you. But let none of you suffer as a murderer or a thief or an evildoer or as a meddler. Yet if anyone suffers as a Christian, let him not be ashamed, but let him glorify God in that name. (1 Peter 4:12–16)

To suffer well is a biblical idea, but in context, we find this passage is encouraging believers as they suffer under persecution or mistreatment, for righteousness' sake (see also 1 Peter 2:20). Christians must be careful not to apply their own ideas of what it looks like to suffer well to the text, demanding others fall in line. That is a form of legalism.

Even if there is application in these passages for all types of suffering, we must remember feeling the emotions of grief is *not* sinful. Jesus himself is called the Man of Sorrows. We will battle various sins (envy, unrighteous anger, self-pity) as we walk through miscarriage. To feel downcast or depressed by the loss of our baby is not one of them. Our weeping is not evidence that we lack faithfulness in our suffering.

Pretend with me that you're an unbeliever who is interested in learning more about Christianity. You have a Christian friend who seems to handle suffering with ease. Whatever is thrown her way rolls right off her back as easily as the words "God is good!" jump from her mouth. She leaves you in awe of her strength.

What you don't see is when she wakes up in a pool of sweat as her body shivers from another panic attack. She hasn't told you that sometimes she wails so hard she begins to feel sick. She feels pressure to put her best face forward so that people won't think ill of her. But all you see is how she doesn't seem to care about the hard circumstances in her life. You wish you didn't care about yours. Maybe if you become a Christian, you'll be happy, like her. But then months after your conversion, you get hit with a hard trial and you're surprised to find that grief and sadness have found you. You begin to wonder if there's something wrong with you. Do you not love the Lord as much as you thought? Maybe you aren't truly saved. Your faith is nearly uprooted, flailing in the wind of these questions.

Do you see how utterly damaging this can be to new believers? Imagine a different scenario. You meet up with your Christian friend for a walk. She is in an ongoing battle with infertility. You ask how she's doing and she says, "This season is really hard; my heart is broken. I long for a baby so deeply. I find myself crying out to Jesus all the time." Instead of leaving the park trail in awe of her ability to be happy in this trial, the conversation leaves you wondering how she trusts God even as her heart aches. You begin to wonder, *Who is this Jesus*? If you do become a Christian, you're equipped with the understanding that suffering and sorrow will come. You might even still experience depression. But God is your Shepherd who carries you through it all. You'll know that you can be incredibly joyful and extremely grieved at the same time. But even if your joy is stolen, you are safe in the arms of your Savior who sustains your faith until the end.

Maybe to suffer well is to be able to admit that the loss of our baby is a horrific grief while also remembering that Jesus is near. Maybe it looks like singing songs of praise to God through tears, even as our hearts shatter. Could it be that what the world needs is to see that grief and joy can intertwine? Or maybe that Christ simply sustains us through it all?

## More than Sanctification

At some point during my losses I found myself thanking God for my miscarriages. I thought that to be faithful in my suffering, I must be thankful for the cause of my grief: losing babies.

In Corrie Ten Boom's memoir, *The Hiding Place*, she shares a story about how her sister, Betsie, encouraged her to thank God for the fleas pestering them in Ravensbruck, a concentration camp during the Holocaust:

"Thank You," Betsie went on serenely, "for the fleas and for—"

The Fleas! This was too much. "Betsie, there's no way even God can make me grateful for a flea."

"'Give thanks in *all* circumstances,'" she quoted. "It doesn't say, 'in pleasant circumstances.' Fleas are part of this place where God has put us."

And so we stood between piers of bunks and gave thanks for fleas.[18]

Many of us read this story and are left in awe of Betsie's faith. I know I would struggle to thank God for fleas as well as many other things in a concentration camp. We might read an account like this, where someone has endured horrendous circumstances and wonder, *Does God expect me to thank him for my circumstances? Does he demand I have gratitude for the loss of my child?* Yet, the Bible verse in question says to give thanks "*in* all circumstances," not *for* all circumstances (1 Thessalonians 5:16–18). This means we can be grateful for what God is doing in our suffering—how he's sustaining our faith, comforting us in our grief, growing us in Christlikeness, and providing for our needs, but we are not required to be thankful that our baby is gone. It may feel radical to thank God for the very source of our suffering, but it isn't necessarily biblical. In fact, Betsie doesn't thank God for the Nazis who were torturing and murdering the Jews. As far as we know, she didn't thank him for the death of her father, either.

Sometimes it seems there are Christians who operate under the assumption that experiencing suffering is good. This might leave us wondering if we are meant to believe the death of our baby is good. Deep down, we know the answer is a resounding *no*. In the Bible, death is described as an enemy. Miscarriage could never be described as good. If you asked most believers, no matter their theological background, they would likely agree. So, where does this idea come from?

There is a beautiful truth found in Romans 8:28. This verse says that God uses everything that comes into our life—including suffering a miscarriage—for our good. This is a great comfort for believers. Unfortunately, humans are masters at adding to God's word. And that's what many have done in the case of this verse.

The "good" here is most commonly interpreted as our sanctification. I wholeheartedly agree with that interpretation. But I think we've simplified it a bit too much. God isn't only concerned with our growth in holiness, but also that we would experience his love, comfort, and faithfulness toward us. This is all part of growing in Christlikeness. When a couple loses their pre-born baby, God is just as concerned about washing over them with his comfort as he is about washing them with his word. Why have so many churches made trials into lessons? Couples are encouraged to be grateful for the loss of their baby because suffering is God's means of sanctification. Tragedies become trophies. The death of our babies, God's goodness to us. Though God is good despite our circumstances; miscarriage is not.

When Christians say, "God is trying to teach you something" as a woman aches over her baby, they place the burden of blame on her shoulders. It may seem like an innocent or even encouraging thought, but let's add some meat to it. For example: "God is trying to teach you patience" turns into "God took my baby because I'm impatient." Some even assume she's sinning: "Once you stop idolizing a baby, God will give you one." Can you feel the heaping shame of these comments? Not only have they brought into question the value of the baby we lost, but they have made hurtful assumptions about the object of our worship.

God did not take our babies to teach us a lesson. God *is* sovereign. He is *not* the author of evil, suffering, and death. We cannot pretend to understand why things like miscarriage happen. I'm not sure we're meant to try. One thing is certain—in the middle of our grief, God will provide his presence. For God draws near to the broken-hearted (Psalm 34:18). It is a precious gift to sense his nearness and be carried through by his steadfast love.

Often, we are encouraged to look for the good in our loss. I'm writing this book to help us see the gifts God gives among the grief of losing our babies. But we don't always have eyes to see the goodness of God in the midst of it. And that's okay. The truth that our suffering isn't wasted is encouraging. But we need not strain our eyes to search for the why of our miscarriage. We can simply rest in the grace of our Lord, the Good Shepherd, knowing we are carried. We are held, even in our unbelief.

## Miscarriage Is Not Good

Dear reader, the loss of your baby is not good. It is a tragedy. Though God does *use* our sorrow for good, he does not *call* the loss of our precious child good. He grieves alongside us. He kneels down to weep with us. Even though Christ's death brought about the most good—our salvation—his brutal murder was horrific. It was tragic. As is the loss of our unborn babies. Sometimes suffering well might look like running to God with our lament and crying out to him in our torment. Sometimes, growth is less about a steady list of works, but a calling out to God in our suffering just like our Savior. This quote by Grant Macaskill about being crucified with Christ (i.e., sanctification) captures this:

> We often participate in the cruciform life, not in glad obedience, but in bewildered suffering. Sometimes disciples resemble Christ the most at the point where they cry "why have you forsaken me?" Cruciformity often looks and feels like defeat.[19]

If the Son lifted his cry to the Father in his suffering, surely it is fitting for mere created beings to cry out to him too. In the hours before his crucifixion Jesus wailed, saying, "My soul is very sorrowful, even to death" (Matthew 26:38). Was Jesus sinning when his soul was cast down in the garden of Gethsemane—when he was so distressed that blood mingled with his sweat (Luke 22:44)? Of course not! We know he lived a perfectly sinless life. After all, Hebrews 4:15 declares, "For we do not have a high priest who is unable to sympathize with our weaknesses, but one who in every respect has been tempted as we are, yet without sin." Jesus experienced downcastness. Are we to presume that we can walk through this life unfazed by sorrow when the perfect Son of God did not?

Yet some continue to hold to a bootstrap theology of suffering where believers respond to grief more like Stoics than children of God. Some people may ignore your grief, explain away your loss, or question your faithfulness. They might wrongly examine if you are suffering well. If that has happened to you, I am so sorry. God is not judging you when tears flow so hard you struggle to sing his praise. He does not expect the news of a friend's pregnancy to not cause gripping pain in your heart. You do not have to search for answers, reasons, or lessons to be learned. You need only to rest in the comforting arms of your good, good Father.

## Psalm of Lament

My tears have been my food
    day and night,
while they say to me all the day long,
    "Where is your God?"
These things I remember,
    as I pour out my soul:
how I would go with the throng
    and lead them in procession to the house of God
with glad shouts and songs of praise,
    a multitude keeping festival.

Why are you cast down, O my soul,
    and why are you in turmoil within me?
Hope in God; for I shall again praise him,
    my salvation and my God. (Psalm 42:3–6a)

## Guided Lament

I can't stop crying, Lord. I miss my baby so much. I feel depressed deep in my soul. Help me to place my hope in you. For Jesus's sake. Amen.

## Bring Your Lament to God:

## Chapter 4

# The Gift of Weakness in Light of Redemption

## *Lord, My Body Betrayed Me*

*I wonder sometimes*
*if there might be three*
*tiny grave-markers*
*in the corners of that unseen place*
*that once held you.*
*A mother's womb turned graveyard;*
*a woman's body turned enemy.*
*What's it like warring with your own self?*
*To wake up hating the vessel, but forced to live in it?*
*Learning to accept that even when I hate my body,*
*God calls it good?*
*Broken.*
*Graveyard.*

*Weak.*
*But God says,*
*Redeemed—already, but not yet.*
*It's just that the not yet sometimes feels like*
*never.*

"*Lord, thank you* for this early birthday gift," my husband prayed, beaming with joy. Two pink lines appeared quickly that evening, showing evidence that our second baby had taken root in my womb. It was only a few months after the loss of our first, and my mind flashed back to labor pains in the hallway and saying "never again." But here I was again, pregnant. Anxious. *Terrified.*

Just over a week later, on my husband's birthday, I began miscarrying our second beloved child. On the following Father's Day, our third baby slipped from my womb as well. Oh, how these dates stung. Two days meant for celebration now held only grief and confusion.

I couldn't give my husband what a wife is supposed to give. Rather than life, my body birthed death. I felt like I failed him. He was a father, but because of my broken body, he had nothing to show for it. *What is wrong with me? Why can't I hold onto our babies?* My womb was created to provide safety and nourishment, but instead it proved to be a hostile environment where babies snuggled in but couldn't stay long. I desperately wanted them to stay. When I received the diagnosis showing that it was indeed *my* body that had prevented their bodies from growing, it felt as if I had killed them with my own hands. My body became my enemy. It betrayed me. It betrayed my babies.

In the confusion of miscarriage, where all we want is answers for the loss, sometimes women may start to blame themselves. This feeling often intensifies if she has lost more than one baby. Many women who experience pregnancy loss find themselves fighting shame and fear regarding their body's struggle to carry their child. We fear we did something wrong. We worry an unknown disorder is causing complications. Maybe we consume too much sugar, or don't eat enough, or forget our vitamins too often. If only we'd eaten healthier, rested more, stayed hydrated, skipped the coffee ... the list goes on. Then there are those of us who hold test results in hand that expose the truth we fear—something in our body really *has* gone amiss. Whether you know the reason for the loss of your unborn child or not, it is easy to feel like your body is at fault, or worse, like *you* are at fault.

## When Our Bodies Became Broken

The truth is, all of our bodies are broken because we're under the curse of the fall. God created all things in heaven and on earth and declared it all good (Genesis 1:31). He created the first two humans, Adam and Eve, out of the dust of the earth, then breathed the breath of life into them. The world around them was perfect. Their bodies, perfect too. They enjoyed unhindered fellowship with God himself. Can you imagine walking with God in the garden?

The sun shining on your unblemished body, leaving no damage, only warmth? Reaching out to touch the mane of a great lion and hearing a purr in return? Fruits of every color dangling low to earth, ripe for picking, never spoiled? Every day was filled with wonder. There was no fear of death or pain or loss. Miscarriage wasn't in their vocabulary. But when Eve opened her ears and therefore her heart to the deceitful serpent, she and her husband took fruit from the only tree withheld from them and ate. Perfection was destroyed. With one rebellious bite, sin and death were ushered into our world.

In Genesis 3:16, the Lord says to Eve, "I will surely multiply your pain in childbearing; in pain you shall bring forth children." The increased pain in bearing children isn't simply a reference to labor pain in a live birth. Heart-wrenching realities like infertility, miscarriage, stillbirth, and infant loss can all be traced back to that moment in the garden. Every day, our eyes observe the effects of sin in the world around us, from the dead plant in the pot outside my back door to the tears I wiped from my Papaw's face as his body succumbed to leukemia. Sin and death surround us. We can't escape the reality that our bodies buckle under the weight of sin's curse.

Women who experience miscarriage are deeply aware of the harshness of this truth. Nothing has roused my mind to the consequences of Genesis 3 like when death took place within my own body. I've never felt the brokenness of this sin-tainted world like I have when labor pains end in empty arms. Maybe for you it was the silence that seemed to fill the room when there should have been a heartbeat. Or the moment you knelt beside your toddler to explain to them that the baby in mommy's belly has gone to be with Jesus. Do you hear it? Creation is *groaning.* And we groan too.

> And not only the creation, but we ourselves, who have the first-fruits of the Spirit, groan inwardly as we wait eagerly for adoption as sons, the redemption of our bodies. (Romans 8:23)

We groan and we wait.

## The Reality of Broken Bodies

In 2 Corinthians 12, we witness a glimpse of the apostle Paul's suffering. To humble him and deepen his trust in the Lord, God allowed a "thorn in the flesh" to torment him. Paul begged the Lord to take his suffering away three times until finally, God answered him with these famous words, "My grace is sufficient for you, for my power is made perfect in weakness." (2 Corinthians 12:9) We're given little information about what Paul's thorn entailed. Was it a literal thorn in his side? Doubtful, but possible. It could have been some kind of chronic illness. Many of us know what that's like. Maybe it wasn't a physical type of suffering at all. Depression is a thorn of suffering millions of people face every day. We can only speculate on what Scripture doesn't clearly state. But one thing is sure, we each have our own thorns.

Losing babies in the womb definitely feels like a thorn sent to torment us. Some of us wonder if it will ever be plucked out of our side. We feel it when another pregnancy announcement pops up, reminding us of the women who seem to have little trouble sustaining a pregnancy. For some, the thorn sinks deeper into our skin as we face another baby gone too soon. It pierces our hearts when the reminder of loss shows up with our monthly cycle. Surely, we understand what it's like to plead with God to heal our bodies and take away our pain. We are women with thorns in our wombs. Women whose bodies feel like graveyards. Women who understand the reality of the brokenness of our own bodies.

It might be tempting to despise this vessel which carries our soul—longing instead to be free of it. But we need not be like the gnostics, believing the body is inherently evil. God created our bodies and called them good. Sin has shrouded that goodness for a time, but when Jesus comes back perfection will be restored. We will be changed, but we will still have our own physical bodies (1 Corinthians 15:42–55). Our hope is not found in casting away our bodies as if they are evil. Our hope is in Christ who will free our bodies from the effects of sin. But right now, we are in the in-between. We are still struggling with a variety of weaknesses.

## Blessed Weakness

Staring sideways at the blank TV, feeling utterly alone, I laid on my couch wondering if I might disappear into the depths of my own sorrow. The wound in my heart was gaping—a pain as deep as a knife could cut. Yet, there was a numbness that washed over me too. A desire to escape, but no working legs to take me away. After losing our second baby I felt paralyzed by grief, unsure if I'd ever find the strength to hope again. In those moments one thing was clear: only God could get me through this; I had no strength left.

The pain we feel in our bodies extends far beyond the day we miscarried. It reaches different parts of the body, including our mind, and can show up as excessive fatigue, anxiety, depression, lack of appetite, and even a struggle to manage daily tasks. While there is a range of different experiences between each woman and miscarriage, one thing is certain: pregnancy loss reveals our humanity; that we are made of dust (Psalm 103:14).

Far be it from me to say that grieving the loss of an unborn baby makes a woman weak. Yet it can make us *feel* weak. The traumatic physical and emotional effects of miscarriage take a toll on us. Hyperventilating and falling to the floor as labor pains pulse through your abdomen makes you feel weak. Holding your tiny baby in the palm of your hand makes you feel helpless. Feeling unable to hold tears back for months can make you feel weak. Losing so much blood certainly makes you feel fragile. And yet, there are blessings in the midst of these feelings and realities of weakness. There are gifts to discover.

When we walk through the grief of miscarriage, we are given the opportunity to experience God's comfort and strength. He brings provision for our needs and carries us through the dusks and dawns of our grief. We taste his grace through experiencing the power of Christ resting on us (2 Corinthians 12:9b). In the fresh moments of our suffering, it may feel hard to sense God's presence with us, and that is normal. There will be a day when we will look back through eyes that have seen him live up to his faithfulness. As his love remains steadfast toward us each day, we will find our roots of trust in him deepen. As we become more rooted in Christ, we will experience the peace of knowing he will never leave us. Through the work of the Holy Spirit we are enabled, even as we suffer through miscarriage, to say with Paul, "I will boast all the more gladly of my weaknesses, so that the power of Christ may rest upon me. For the sake of Christ, then, I am content with weaknesses ... For when I am weak, then I am strong!" (2 Corinthians 12:9b–10). We are carried through the storm of miscarriage by the strength of the God who calms raging storms.

Possibly the most beautiful blessing within the gift of weakness is that it beckons us to fix our eyes on eternity, where all that is broken will be healed. Chromosomal abnormalities, clotting disorders, hormonal disruptions, genetic defects, and other causes of pregnancy loss will vanish. Sin's effects on our bodies and the bodies of our babies will be swallowed up at the coming of Christ. One day, dear sisters, our bodies will be redeemed.

## The Redemption of Our Bodies

In the eighth chapter of Romans, written by the apostle Paul, we find comforting truths for women walking through miscarriage. The well-known verse reminding us that "God works all things for our good" is often quoted to Christians in the midst of a trial (v. 28). But that verse is part of a bigger, more beautiful promise.

After recalling our adoption by the Father and the truth that we will one day be glorified with our Savior, Paul reminds us that the suffering we experience in this world isn't worth comparing with the glory to come (v. 18). In another epistle he calls them "momentary afflictions":

> For this light momentary affliction is preparing for us an eternal weight of glory beyond all comparison, as we look not to the things that are seen but to the things that are unseen. For the things that are seen are transient, but the things that are unseen are eternal. (2 Corinthians 4:17–18)

How could he believe that? This man, who suffered multiple beatings, shipwrecks, persecution, and similar suffering claims the trials of this life are *momentary*. The grief that enters our life when our bodies struggle to sustain a pregnancy doesn't feel momentary, does it? But even this piercing pain is a momentary affliction in light of what awaits us—in light of eternity with Jesus.

Paul goes on in Romans 8 to explain how creation groans, waiting for the pain caused by sin to cease and eternity to begin. He encourages us that, as we groan over the heartbreak and confusion of this life, as we feel the cramping of death inside us, as we weep at the throne of God—void of words—the Spirit helps us in our weakness, interceding for us (v. 26). He translates our groans into words of lament and worship, prayer and praise to the God who gives and takes away.

Finally, Paul declares "those whom he predestined he also called, and those whom he called he also justified, and those whom he justified he also *glorified*" (v. 30, emphasis mine).

As Adam was formed from the dust, so are we. But those in Christ will be resurrected as he was, trading in our weak, perishable bodies for a body that bears the image of heaven. We'll trade in dishonor for glory, weakness for power (1 Corinthians 15:42–49). We will put off this sin-afflicted mortal body and put on a glorified one, free of sin's curse and join in the chorus: "Death is swallowed up in victory. O death, where is your victory? O death, where is your sting?" (1 Corinthians 15:54b–55).

One day, our groans will end. On that day, we will stand in glorified bodies beholding the glory of our Savior, and every ounce of our sorrow will be wiped away (Revelation 21:4). This is our hope. This is what we recall when our eyes are swollen with grief and our bodies ache with loss. You and I can allow our weaknesses—whatever they are—to point our eyes heavenward, fixing them on Christ. One glorious day, we will appear with him in glory.

> If then you have been raised with Christ, seek the things that are above, where Christ is, seated at the right hand of God. Set your minds on things that are above, not on things that are on earth. For you have died, and your life is hidden with Christ in God. When Christ who is your life appears, then you also will appear with him in glory. (Colossians 3:1–3)

Human sin brought death into the world, destroying the perfection of Eden and damaging our bodies, but Jesus defeated the power of sin and death when he died upon a cross and rose again. And he doesn't simply restore what was lost—no, he makes everything *new.*

So we do not lose heart. Though our outer self is wasting away, our inner self is being renewed day by day (2 Corinthians 4:16). Look up. You may feel weak, but your Savior is mighty in strength.

## Psalm of Lament

Be gracious to me, O Lord, for I am in distress;
    my eye is wasted from grief;
    my soul and my body also.
For my life is spent with sorrow,
    and my years with sighing;
my strength fails because of my iniquity,
    and my bones waste away. (Psalm 31:9–10)

## Guided Lament

Lord, the physical effects of grief are weighing me down. My eyes hurt, my joints ache, and the stress is making me sick. I have no more strength. Help me. Amen.

## Bring Your Lament to God:

Chapter 5

# The Gift of Experiencing God's Peace

## *Lord, I'm Afraid of the Future*

*I wonder if*
*we're all just*
*trying to look brave*
*when*
*bravery is more like*
*taking hold of Jesus's robe;*
*clinging,*
*crying,*
*courageously begging.*

"*I just have a feeling* we'll lose more babies."

The words didn't shock me as they fled from my mouth. I'd been feeling this way for a while and only just shared it with my husband. When should we try for another baby? That was the question floating in the air around us. The question neither of us really knew the answer to. My sweet husband tried to comfort me with statistics and truths about how feelings aren't always in line with reality. But I simply couldn't shake the persistent thoughts of impending grief. I couldn't suppress the memories of writhing in pain in the hallway or holding my baby in the palm of my hand. My husband couldn't promise me these things wouldn't happen again. No one could.

Only one to two percent of women who miscarry have repeated miscarriages.[20] Even after one miscarriage, the predicted chance of miscarrying a second time is only about twenty percent.[21] Due to the commonality of miscarrying one child and then going on to experience a live birth shortly after, many women are optimistic after their first loss. I was not one of them. I had growing anxiety—an overwhelming dreadful feeling that my story would be different—that there was more trauma to come. I was afraid of it, squinting to peer into the deep inky darkness that seemed to lurk just ahead of me.

Maybe you're feeling optimistic about the future. What a gift it is to look ahead without fear. But I know there are some of you who, like I did, feel a little apprehensive about what is to come.

*What if I miscarry again?*

*What if I experience stillbirth in the next pregnancy?*

*What if I face infertility after loss?*

*What if I only lose babies?*

*What if I fall into depression?*
*What if I'm unbearably anxious next time?*
*What if I have to have a D&C?*
*What if I experience another hemorrhage?*

The what ifs can be deafening; the worries of the future, paralyzing. Because, the truth is, it's possible these things might happen to any of us. We live in a broken world where sin's effects have stretched as deep as a mother's womb. Women who've experienced miscarriage know this all too well. So what do we do with these fears, feelings, and realities? How can we take steps of faith as we face the future?

## God is Worthy of Our Trust

Many people are quick to tell us to trust God, but it's hard to trust a God we don't really know. Some of us are learning for the first time who God is, while others need to be refreshed by truths they have forgotten. I had trouble at times trusting the Lord through our miscarriages. Something clicked as I began to view him not as a harsh God, hurrying me through my grief, but instead as a loving Father who wept with me. This truth about him makes all the difference in our grieving.

To fully comprehend the Almighty God is a task unattainable by our frail human minds, but when we are afraid, it helps to go back to the basics of who God is, by looking to his word. There, we find truths about his character that help us see how much he can be trusted.

So, who is he? Who is the God of Scripture? He's the Good Shepherd.

> I am the good shepherd. The good shepherd lays down his life for the sheep. (John 10:11)

He's the God of hope who can fill us with joy and peace.

> May the God of hope fill you with all joy and peace in believing, so that by the power of the Holy Spirit you may abound in hope. (Romans 15:13)

He is faithful; his love toward us is steadfast.

> Your steadfast love, O LORD, extends to the heavens,
> your faithfulness to the clouds. (Psalm 36:5)

He is good.

> Oh, how abundant is your goodness,
> which you have stored up for those who fear you and
> worked for those who take refuge in you,
> in the sight of the children of mankind! (Psalm 31:19)

He is sovereign.

> For I am God, and there is no other;
> I am God, and there is none like me,
> declaring the end from the beginning
> and from ancient times things not yet done,

saying, "My counsel shall stand,
  and I will accomplish all my purpose,"
calling a bird of prey from the east,
  the man of my counsel from a far country.
I have spoken, and I will bring it to pass;
  I have purposed, and I will do it. (Isaiah 46:9b–11)

His works are good.

> You are good and do good. (Psalm 119:68a)

He is with us in affliction.

> When you pass through the waters, I will be with you;
>   and through the rivers, they shall not overwhelm you;
> when you walk through fire you shall not be burned,
>   and the flame shall not consume you. (Isaiah 43:2)

He will never forsake us.

> It is the LORD who goes before you. He will be with you; he will not leave you or forsake you. Do not fear or be dismayed. (Deuteronomy 31:8; see also Hebrews 13:5)

He provides for all our needs.

> And my God will supply every need of yours according to his riches in glory in Christ Jesus. (Philippians 4:19)

He is a safe place for us to take refuge.

> The LORD is my rock and my fortress and my deliverer,
> my God, my rock, in whom I take refuge,
> my shield, and the horn of my salvation, my stronghold.
> (Psalm 18:2)

He is the God of comfort.

> Blessed be the God and Father of our Lord Jesus Christ, the Father of mercies and God of all comfort, who comforts us in all our affliction, so that we may be able to comfort those who are in any affliction, with the comfort with which we ourselves are comforted by God. (2 Corinthians 1:3–4)

Our God is patient, gracious, merciful, and kind (Psalm 86:15). He's holy, omniscient (all-knowing), omnipotent (all-powerful), wise, infinite, self-sufficient, omnipresent (always everywhere), just, and unchangeable (Psalm 99:9; Psalm 147:5; Romans 11:33; Colossians 1:17; John 5:26; Jeremiah 23:23–24; Deuteronomy 32:4; Malachi 3:6). I could fill this entire book with words about who God is and it would be like handing you one bloom in an endless field of wildflowers. You must open the Bible yourself. Within it, we are given all the truths we need to prove God is trustworthy.

## Is He Worthy?

Scripture teaches us to trust God because he is worthy of our trust. We know that, in him, there is no darkness (1 John 1:5). His inerrant word says he does not lie (Numbers 23:19; Hebrews 6:18). He never changes and will never forsake his people (Hebrews 13:8;

Psalm 9:10). His word stands forever (Isaiah 40:8). Most astonishingly, he remains faithful when we are faithless (2 Timothy 2:13). God is good to us, and he has promised good to us. We have a beautiful inheritance in Christ, and all of the promises of God find their "yes and Amen" in the Son (Ephesians 1:3–14; 2 Corinthians 1:20).

How beautiful is it that, even when we feel void of faith in God and his promises, even when we have lost hope, he doesn't turn his back on us? He doesn't chastise us when we're scared of facing another traumatic emergency room visit. No disappointment enters his heart when a panic attack ripples through our body when pregnant after loss. He simply remains faithful because his love toward us is based not on who we are or how well we trust him, but who *he* is, and he doesn't change.

The admonition to "Trust in the Lord!" is everywhere in Scripture. It's unavoidable. Even so, when faced with losing a baby to miscarriage, our trust can (and often does) waver. How do you trust the Lord when blood appears on the toilet paper *again? Or* when a heartbeat can't be found? Can a woman trust God when her milk comes in but there's no baby to nurse? How do you trust a sovereign God when after days, weeks, or even months of dreaming about meeting your son or daughter, you're left only with the memory of how it felt to envelop them in your womb? Due dates pass, your belly flattens, and your heart throbs with agony. Can God really be trusted? Is he worthy? Yes, he is. He is worthy, yet we are dust. And his worthiness—his righteousness—covers all our shortcomings. This frees us up to trust him, however imperfect our trust might be.

Have you ever opened up to a friend about your fears? Maybe you shared about how scared you are of losing another baby or your fear that you won't be able to conceive again after all this loss. You were longing for comfort. But they responded with what feels like more of a rebuke than encouragement: "Don't worry. You just need to trust God."

It is true we have every reason to trust God in pregnancy loss, but this response leaves us feeling hushed and shamed. What if, instead of a command, God has weaved these reminders to trust him into his word as an *encouragement* to his children? While some Christians leave little room for wrestling, God beckons us to wrestle with him like Jacob did (Genesis 32:22–32). We bring our fears and desires to our Father, contending with him in prayer. And he does not run or waver.

## I Believe, Help My Unbelief

Trusting in God doesn't mean every fear will lift from our shoulders. In fact, it would be odd to not carry some amount of concern when faced with fears like being threatened with another miscarriage. When I was fourteen weeks pregnant with my fourth child, I began spotting. This is how miscarriage began for me every time, so I panicked. I sobbed. I lamented. I *begged*. I had made it past the twelve week mark when suddenly my worst fear was clawing at my back. I drove to the obstetrician flooding my car with tears.

*God, I can't handle another loss. If I lose this baby, you have to carry me through.*

Trusting God means facing real fears and bringing them to him for help. Psalm 46:1 says, "God is our refuge and strength, a very present help in trouble." It would be unnatural to no longer care about the potential loss of another baby. But, as Christians, we can find peace in the fury of our fears by taking refuge in God.

Trusting him can look like running to him with our fearful thoughts, too. During all of my pregnancies, bathrooms became battlefields where I would pray, *Lord, please sustain the life of my baby.* This prayer must have been on my lips a million times. From the moment a woman is threatened with a miscarriage to the months and years after she loses her baby, various fears plague her mind. Emergency rooms can trigger panic. The sight of menstrual blood can bring up traumatic memories of waking up to untimely contractions. *"Lord, help me through this visit to the doctor." "God, free me from the memories of hemorrhaging and the panic they induce." "Please God, give me peace about the future. I don't want to lose more babies."* God never tires of our requests. We have the freedom and privilege to cast our cares on the Lord—all of them—as often as they come (1 Peter 5:7). Psalm 62:8 says, "Trust in him at all times, O people; pour out your heart before him; God is a refuge for us." Trusting God includes pouring our hearts out to him.

Sometimes trusting him as we walk through miscarriage simply means having confidence that he will carry us through to the other side of all our fears. We don't know how, but we know *Who*. God has always been faithful to us and always will be. Meditating on his character and promises helps us experience peace in the midst of fears like walking through infertility, recurrent pregnancy loss, being probed and poked for testing, physical trauma, and other very real fears that miscarriage can stir up. We may not know the immediate future, but we know for certain that in the end we will be in heaven with Jesus and with our precious babies lost to miscarriage. We have an eternal hope that anchors the soul, even as our mind and body feel unstable (Hebrews 6:18–19). God will carry us through any and all fears we might face.

Yet, sometimes we struggle to believe that. If we didn't experience doubts we wouldn't be human. There once was a man whose son was ravaged by a demon. In desperation, this father begged Jesus to have compassion on them and rescue his son from his torment. He spoke potentially the most relatable words ever spoken, asking for not just the miracle itself but for Jesus's help in believing it (Mark 9:14–27). Just like that father we cry out, "I believe, help my unbelief!" We say, "God, I want to believe you are good, I want to believe you are trustworthy, help me." The Spirit will help us, for he is called Helper (John 14:26). He points us to truths about Jesus and fills our hearts with his peace. He helps us rest even as fears linger on, because ultimately, we know he prepares a table for us in the presence of our enemies (Psalm 4:8; Psalm 23:5). We can sit and eat, encouraged that he is near, his plans are good, and we have an eternal hope that cannot be stolen. We grieve, but we can grieve as those who have hope, because we do (1 Thessalonians 4:13). We will dwell in the house of the Lord forever, and all fears will be relieved, and every grief healed.

## You are Carried

Those feelings and fears about losing more babies eventually became my reality. I went on to lose two more unborn children. It was heavy; the grief was like trying to bear up under the weight of a semi-truck. Though we lost our sweet babies, I was met with grace from above I didn't expect. I was carried through my deepest fears on a river of God's steadfast love.

I wish I could claim that after reading the words in this chapter you will feel free from your fears and anxieties. But that's simply not within my power. My hope is that you will close these pages knowing that no matter what lies in your future, God promises to carry you through it all.

We named our first baby Amos, which means "carried by God." I chose this name because my precious child is safe in the arms of God. But I also chose it because I was too, as I walked through losing him and the grief of never holding him myself. Even now, the pain still stings as I write, wishing I could snuggle him in my arms and kiss his little nose. I was—I am—carried through it all.

Dear reader, he will carry you too, through every single tear and trial, every gut-wrenching moment where grief swallows the air in your lungs. You are carried by God. Believe it. Spirit, help us believe.

## Psalm of Lament

I cry aloud to God,
aloud to God, and he will hear me.
In the day of my trouble I seek the Lord;
in the night my hand is stretched out without wearying;
my soul refuses to be comforted.
When I remember God, I moan;
when I meditate, my spirit faints. *Selah*

You hold my eyelids open;
I am so troubled that I cannot speak.
I consider the days of old,
the years long ago.
I said, "Let me remember my song in the night;
let me meditate in my heart."
Then my spirit made a diligent search:
"Will the Lord spurn forever,
and never again be favorable?
Has his steadfast love forever ceased?
Are his promises at an end for all time?
Has God forgotten to be gracious?
Has he in anger shut up his compassion?" *Selah*

Then I said, "I will appeal to this,
to the years of the right hand of the Most High."

I will remember the deeds of the LORD;
yes, I will remember your wonders of old.

I will ponder all your work,
and meditate on your mighty deeds.
Your way, O God, is holy.
What god is great like our God?

You are the God who works wonders;
you have made known your might among the peoples.
(Psalm 77:1–14)

## Guided Lament

Father, I need your help. My spirit is so troubled I can barely find words, but you know my grief. You know how my heart aches for my baby. I feel no comfort in this. Great Comforter, please pour out your comfort on me. For Jesus's sake. Amen.

## Bring Your Lament to God:

Chapter 6

# The Gift of Our Good Shepherd

## *Lord, Your Goodness and Mercy Follow Me*

*A single tear*
*Drips*
*on the bed*
*as I stare at the white wall we painted when I felt hopeful.*

*Depression is a funny thing;*
*you don't always see it coming.*
*But it comes*
*crashing*
*like those waves at the Outer Banks*
*that almost drowned me.*
*We laugh about it now,*
*how silly I looked running from the shore.*
*But it scared me.*

*And so does this.*
*So does this.*

*It was a warm October* that year. As the leaves began to boast one last time, bearing auburns and oranges before falling to their death, I suspected new life. The first signs of pregnancy found their place in the smell of a far-off unlit candle and the heaviness of my eyes. One pregnancy test later and my suspicions were confirmed.

Upon my heart laid the weighty fear of loss. My husband dared to hope—to rejoice in this little life newly nestled in my womb—I, however, wasn't so brave. I held this pregnancy, this precious baby, at arms' length. Instead of resting in my Good Shepherd's embrace, I tried to protect myself from the incredible grief that inevitably comes when a woman loses a baby to miscarriage. I sought to distance myself emotionally from the pregnancy. The thought of losing another unborn child crippled me. I knew God would carry me through. I believed it with everything in me. Yet I couldn't fathom more loss inside my own body. I couldn't imagine the life of another baby slipping silently from my womb again. It was the beginning of questions like, "Will all my babies die?" or "What if I can't *have* children?"

At six weeks pregnant, these questions became reality. Before my eyes, laid the stark contrast of red against white toilet paper, confirming what I already knew in my heart. My baby was gone. I was miscarrying *again*.

The contractions came on as I was showering, lowering my blood pressure and rendering me unable to speak—to call out for help. There would be many more moments like this to come in the future. Moments where I wished to melt away, sliding down into the drain and out of this life rather than being alive and awake to its heartache.

After losing this baby, I sank into the quicksand of depression for a time. The trauma of losing two babies and the hormonal shifts that came with them had taken their toll. I was physically, mentally, emotionally, and spiritually spent. Prior to my losses, I hadn't spent much time pondering Jesus as the Good Shepherd. I hadn't thought about sheep or shepherding at all really. In the Gospel of John, Jesus refers to himself over and over again as the "good shepherd." As the shaking arms of my heart began to grasp the beauty of what this meant for me in my suffering, I found the rest I desperately needed. In my sorrow, I clung to my Good Shepherd. I knew he would hold me close to himself as a sheep with injured legs, carrying me down this path. I was broken, but I was safe. Friend, if you are in Christ, you are part of his fold. You are carried. You are safe in the arms of your Shepherd.

## A Shepherd and His Sheep

Throughout the Old Testament, the idea of God being a shepherd to his people is not hard to find. Psalm 100:3 declares, "Know that the Lord, he is God! It is he who made us, and we are his; we are his people, and the sheep of his pasture." But one of the clearest examples is found in the shepherd-king, David (Ezekiel 37:24). When God, through the prophet Samuel, seeks David out to be King over Israel, where is he found? Out shepherding his flock, for he was a shepherd. It's fitting then, that David wrote Psalm 23, which beautifully depicts the Lord as our shepherd. Who better than a man who was living out the very analogy of which he wrote?

> The LORD is my shepherd; I shall not want.
>     He makes me lie down in green pastures.
> He leads me beside still waters.
>     He restores my soul.
> He leads me in paths of righteousness
>     for his name's sake.
>
> Even though I walk through the valley of the shadow of death,
>     I will fear no evil,
> for you are with me;
>     your rod and your staff,
>     they comfort me.
>
> You prepare a table before me
>     in the presence of my enemies;
> you anoint my head with oil;
>     my cup overflows.
> Surely goodness and mercy shall follow me
>     all the days of my life,
> and I shall dwell in the house of the LORD
>     forever. (Psalm 23)

In this psalm, we find that God gives us rest, provides for us, leads us, protects us, comforts us, and is with us. These truths remain for our entire lives until he brings us into heaven, where "the Lamb in the midst of the throne will be their shepherd, and he will guide them to springs of living water, and God will wipe away every tear from their eyes" (Revelation 7:17).

You are a sheep of the Good Shepherd. I understand how hard it might be to believe this right now, in the middle of the ache of losing your baby. Maybe you feel like it's true for others but not for you. Maybe you feel like a forgotten sheep, as I did at times. Sometimes, it isn't until we make it through a storm that we have eyes to see that God was the one who carried us the whole way. That he never left our side. That he is ever faithful.

I love the ending of Psalm 77. It says, "Your way was through the sea, your path through the great waters; yet your footprints were unseen. You led your people like a flock by the hand of Moses and Aaron." (vv. 19–20). In context, this passage speaks of when God led Israel through the Red Sea, delivering them from their enemies. But we too can take comfort in these words. God is with us as we cross the Red Sea of miscarriage. He is paving the way, even if his footprints are unseen—even when we don't feel his presence. Jesus is our Shepherd, and the Shepherd is *good*.

## The Shepherd is Good

We know that Jesus declared himself to be the *Good Shepherd*. But what exactly does that mean? What comfort does it offer us as we face pregnancy loss? My hope is that, in pondering this analogy and its implications for those of us who experience miscarriage, you will walk away knowing you are held by God, even when it doesn't feel like it.

*The Good Shepherd laid down his life for us:* "I am the good shepherd. The good shepherd lays down his life for the sheep." (John 10:11) Throughout the Gospel of John, we are told that Jesus is seeking out his sheep for the purpose of saving them through sacrificing himself. This is true for every man or woman who has trusted in Christ alone to save them. He laid down his life for *us*. What greater love could there be? (Romans 5:8; John 15:13).

*The Good Shepherd carries his sheep near to his heart:* "He will tend his flock like a shepherd; he will gather the lambs in his arms; he will carry them in his bosom" (Isaiah 40:11a). We are held close to the very heart of our Savior. The same God who kneels down to weep with us picks us up and carries us through every trial and tragedy. When our strength seems to slip away with the child we lost, he scoops us up in his arms, tending to our wounds and bringing us rest.

*The Good Shepherd gently leads us:* "and gently leads those that are with young." (Isaiah 40:11b). If this verse is used to encourage mamas of little ones, surely, it is for those of us who've lost our young too. He gently leads us through the joys and the sorrows of motherhood, and this certainly includes miscarriage. From the moment two pink lines form on a test to when we hear the ultrasound tech quietly say, "I'm so sorry. There's no heartbeat," he goes before us. We are not alone in the valley of the shadow of death (Psalm 23:4).

*The Good Shepherd knows us intimately:* "I am the good shepherd. I know my own and my own know me." (John 10:14). You and I are intimately known by our Good Shepherd. He knows how your arms ache with longing for the baby you never got to hold. He knows how the reactions of others to your grief have pressed in on a tender wound. Nothing is hidden from him—no tear you've cried, question you've grappled with, or wave of grief that nearly drowned you. He sees all. He knows your pain. He knows *you.*

*The Good Shepherd gives us eternal life and protects us:* "I give them eternal life, and they will never perish, and no one will snatch them out of my hand." (John 10:28). Most astounding, Jesus paid the price with his life so that we would live with him in eternity. He protects our faith from all things which might try to snatch it away. He will sustain us through our grief and throughout our whole life, bringing us safe into glory.

Our Shepherd is good. He is compassionate, kind, gentle, and wise. He protects, sustains, comforts, and carries us. In these truths about Jesus, we find we are held, head above the waters that try to rush upon our soul. The grief we feel after losing our baby—vast and deep as the ocean itself—is under the submission of our good God. It may try to swallow up our faith, but Jesus is both the giver, and the sustainer of our faith. We can rest in him as we face the sorrow of miscarriage.

It may feel as though these things cannot be true in your grief. Sometimes God carries us through as we panic in his arms or even as we grow numb to everything around us. Asaph, the writer of

Psalm 77, wrote, "my soul refuses to be comforted" as he reached out for the Lord in his distress (v. 2). In Lamentations, Jeremiah speaks of being "bereft of peace" (3:17a). It is normal to feel downcast and even abandoned when experiencing suffering like miscarriage. But I want you to know that God has not left you, weary saint. He never will. He will always keep his sheep. And if he is good, then he only has good plans for us.

## The Good Shepherd and His Good Plans

On one particular Sunday after my first pregnancy loss, the heaviness of grief bowed me down low. With tears in my eyes, I read the lyrics to the worship song on the screen: "Surely, goodness and mercy shall follow me all the days of my life."[23] I didn't open my lips to sing them for fear of what sorrowful sound might leap from my mouth. In the wake of our loss, I was struggling to believe the truth of those words.

Sometimes, we wrestle with believing that God's plans are good. When I thought about this while weeping over our first unborn baby, I pondered before God ... *even this day, Lord?* I wondered how it could be possible to face the loss of a child and believe goodness and mercy still filled that day. It's possible, but only because of Jesus. This doesn't mean our days, weeks, months, or even years of loss are void of sorrow. It simply means that even in the midst of our grief, goodness and mercy still abound. This is only because of Christ, in whom is all our hope. We can rejoice in him while also feeling deep pain in our hearts over our sweet baby.

The Good Shepherd has plans for us, and his plans are good and merciful—plans meant to lead us to righteousness and deeper communion with him (Psalm 23:3). This is not to say that losing our baby is good. God hates death. We live in a post-fall world where evil happens all around us. And God is not the author of evil. There is great mystery in God's sovereign plans and our suffering. To pretend I have all the answers in this area would be a facade. What I do know is this: in our loss, we lose so much, and we also gain so much. We are given the opportunity to know Jesus more intimately, and this is a good and merciful gift. The loss of our baby is not good, and we can praise the God who gives good gifts in spite of loss. Surely, the Good Shepherd's plans are good. We can trust him. He goes before us and he will see us through.

## The Good Shepherd Who Goes Before Us

Have you ever experienced an obvious work of the Spirit in your life or the life of someone you know? Moments where it would be impossible to deny that God was working? Times where there is no question about it—God went before you, paving the very paths you now walked?

Months before losing our first baby, when my husband and I decided it was time to grow our family, fear entangled my thoughts. No rose-colored glasses settled on the bridge of my nose; I was well aware of the risks that came with trying to conceive. Fears of miscarriage, infertility, still-birth, and even hyperemesis gravidarum all hung in the backdrop of my mind. We were stepping into a new world, opening ourselves up to harsh realities, and I was bracing myself.

To fight anxiety, I committed Psalm 23:6 to memorization. While it was one of many passages I sought to fill my mind with, it was one I continued to come back to. I felt the importance of the truth hidden in this verse. I knew I needed to learn it, believe it, and rehearse it to myself daily. What I was unsure of was, *why*?

Why was the Holy Spirit beckoning me to hide this verse deep in my heart? Why did it seem to jump out at me as if to get my attention? I now recognize God was preparing my heart for the journey through grief my husband and I were about to begin. For the truths in this very psalm would be used by God over and over again to anchor my faith. God had gone before us, and he had pushed through the brush, making a path to the other side. He has paved every path we will walk and is present with us throughout our journey.

## Our Ever-Present Shepherd

The same hot, sunny, Sunday afternoon where I pondered the lyrics of the worship song that had pricked my heart, we came home to see a big brown box on our doorstep. This unexpected gift from an online friend held item after item that pointed to Psalm 23. God saw. God sees. And dear friend, he cares. Not just for me, but for *you*—for every one of his children. He goes before us. The package I received that day, with its mug and Bible study and verse cards, was one way throughout our miscarriage years that God proved to me his goodness and his presence in my suffering. He was there, comforting me, through every silent shower cry, every pregnancy symptom that faded, and every fear that came true. He never left, even when I felt incredibly alone.

He is with you. He is an ever-present help to the couple facing miscarriage (Psalm 46:1). Our Good Shepherd takes us into his arms and carries us. This is important to remember when experiencing the grief upon grief of losing a baby. Our God is not far off. No, he is very near, strengthening us in each moment.

Grief has a way of acting as an overcast sky, making it hard to see the goodness of the Son. We can learn to peer through the fog of pain to the ways he is showing us his goodness even as we grieve. It may be through the prayers of our church family, a friend who brings a meal, or a family member who cries with us. Maybe his goodness is in the wildflowers in your backyard or the silent winter snow or the promise of spring. God might be providing through your husband as he takes care of your other children so you can rest or through your mom who cleans your home. In all of these things, God is telling us, "I am near. I am with you." The shepherd David reminds us,

> Even though I walk through the valley of the shadow of death,
> I will fear no evil,
> for *you are with me*;
> your rod and your staff,
> they comfort me. (Psalm 23:4, *emphasis mine*)

Our Good Shepherd is with us. When we face our greatest fears or most gut-wrenching moments, we can cast ourselves upon him, knowing he cares for us (1 Peter 5:7). When the baby clothes at Target cause our heart to shatter all over again, we can take refuge in God (Psalm 46:1). Under his care, we will be comforted, for he is the God of all comfort (2 Corinthians 1:3). He is with us and promises never to leave (Hebrews 13:5). Let this truth sink in and bring with it deep peace and comfort. When you grieve for your baby, you are not alone. Your ever-present Good Shepherd is weeping alongside you.

In the years of walking through the grief of our miscarriages, I developed the habit of writing out Scripture and prayers to God. It was healing for me to sit in the sunshine on warm days or look out the window in the winter and see his goodness in his creation while journaling his word back to him. I encourage you to make space to sit down for a few moments and do the same. I believe he will meet you there.

## Psalm of Lament

With my voice I cry out to the LORD;
    with my voice I plead for mercy to the LORD.
I pour out my complaint before him;
    I tell my trouble before him.
When my spirit faints within me,
    you know my way! (Psalm 142:1–3a)

## Guided Lament

Lord, I can't believe my baby is gone. It feels so wrong. It is wrong. Death has stolen so much from me. Please be merciful to me, Lord. I am hurting. Amen.

## Bring Your Lament to God:

## Chapter 7

# The Gift of His Word

## *Lord, If Your Word Was Not My Delight...*

*My husband held me in the hallway as*
*labor pains ushered in loss.*
*I held my affliction in my hands;*
*a protest to God, a question: Why?*
*Surely, if his word was not my delight,*
*I'd have perished.*
*I'd have sunk deep into the crevices of grief,*
*never to be seen again.*

*In the morning hours*, I sipped my coffee, sitting on our old brown couch. Before me, my Bible lay open to a New Testament epistle. I picked up my pen and tried to wrap my brain around themes, author intent, and context, but it was as if a cloud of smoke hovered over me, choking out all the brain power I once had. I'm a Bible study nerd at heart. I adore digging into hard passages and seeking to discover the truths therein. But after the loss of each baby, I found my mind was no longer up to the task.

It was the season of the Psalms—the miscarriage years. Every time I strayed to a different part of the Bible, I was overtaken by another wave of loss, tossing me back among pages where the tips of my fingers had grown accustomed. Muscle memory led me there—to highlights and handwritten prayers. Places I'd fought to believe what I was reading with salt-streaked cheeks; evidence of rebellion against my own doubts.

Sometimes the sorrow brought on by my miscarriages threatened to swallow me whole. But it was there, in grief upon grief, that I found myself carried through by God. It was as if he'd scooped me up and placed me on his word. The Scriptures were, to me, a ship of refuge, keeping me afloat upon the waves of loss.

## God Draws Near Through His Word

If you peeked into my Bible today, you'd find prayers and notes in the margins, written in desperation to believe the very words I was scribbling down. Prayers like this one:

> Father, my heart aches for my babies. I long to know them and hold them. But I trust you. Please continue to cause me to treasure Jesus more. Give me grace to prove faithful as I walk this road. Guard my heart against bitterness, envy, resentment. Help me to rejoice with others. And please, grant us babies we can hold and teach your Word. Whatever you choose, it is well with my soul. Amen.

Though I mostly camped out in the Psalms, I wrote this prayer after reading in 1 Samuel about Hannah, who experienced barrenness. Scripture says "she was deeply distressed and prayed to the Lord and wept bitterly" (1 Samuel 1:10). This was one of many passages where God met me in my grief. To be honest, though I did trust God, I struggled to believe his plans were truly better than mine. It was sometimes hard to believe he was good in the face of debilitating contractions or the sight of blood. I wrestled, wondering: was he good to me when I grieved my third baby in a year? There were times when it truly wasn't *well with my soul.* I was a woman, like Hannah, in deep distress. I knew what it meant to weep bitterly.

Yet, throughout these struggles I often experienced the presence of God as he drew me to passages of Scripture that spoke to my soul the exact words I needed. At pivotal times, he provided reminders of his character, of his goodness, and grace. When others questioned my sorrow, God comforted me through his word, showing me examples of how barrenness was a grief worthy of my tears. When I was tempted to sin, the Spirit gently led me to passages that convicted my heart. All of this made it evident God was my very present help and hope.

He will do the same for every woman or couple walking through pregnancy loss. God promises to speak through his word. The two main ways we can seek to hear from him are by opening the Bible ourselves and by hearing it preached at our local church. These are the places we go when we want—*need*—to hear from him: the

Bible in our hands and the Bible preached from the pulpit. When we read Scripture, we are reading the very words of God written to his people, that we may know him and be built up in Christ.

Second Timothy says, "All Scripture is breathed out by God and profitable for teaching, for reproof, for correction, and for training in righteousness, that the man of God may be complete, equipped for every good work" (2 Timothy 3:16–17). But God's word does more than that; he uses it to bring comfort to his suffering children too. God draws near to us through his word as we face the heartache of pregnancy loss.

## We Need His Word

When we are suffering a miscarriage, we are prime targets for the enemy. He seeks to steal our eyes away from Christ, kill the joy of our salvation, and destroy our trust in our Maker. Satan can never take our faith, as it is fully sustained by our Savior who will carry us through like sheep to the pastures of Heaven, but he can tempt us to fix our eyes on our painful circumstances instead of the things above (Colossians 3:1–3). He will work hard to cause us to doubt the goodness of God. He will be most pleased if we forsake running to our heavenly Father in our grief and run instead to things that numb or distract (television, social media, alcohol, etc.). Satan wants to keep our broken hearts broken. He doesn't want us offering them up to the God who heals. Finding hope in God's word? The enemy will do all he can to hinder that endeavor.

There's a reason Satan is often referred to as crafty. He's sneaky—known for twisting God's word. We witness him doing this in the garden when he tempted Eve and in the wilderness when he tempted Jesus. Both times, he twisted and added to God's words, and he continues with this tactic today. He's the author of lies, but his lies are often disguised as truth.

The Bible tells us that God gives his children good gifts (Psalm 84:11; Matthew 7:11). As I lost baby after baby in the womb, Satan tempted me to question if I truly was a child of God. Maybe I had deceived myself into believing he was my Father. Like he did with me, Satan might taunt other women walking through miscarriage by bringing into question their place in God's kingdom. Doesn't God promise good things to his children (Matthew 7:11)? Then why did I lose my baby? We know the answer is that we live in a fallen world, tainted by sin's curse. We know that sometimes God gives us gifts in the midst of sorrow and suffering. Praise God that we know one day he will redeem all things and death will die.

The schemes of the devil don't stop there. He might try to persuade us to believe passages like "Rejoice always!" mean that if we grieve, we lack faith (Philippians 4:4). But truly, believers can be deeply grieved while their faith in God is strong. We must be on guard against the deceit of the devil. We know he prowls around looking for ways to harm the children of God. We know he flings fiery darts in our direction. The Bible is our sword in the battle. He has provided armor to protect us.

> Finally, be strong in the Lord and in the strength of his might. Put on the whole armor of God, that you may be able to stand against the schemes of the devil. For we do not wrestle against flesh and blood, but against the rulers, against the authorities, against the cosmic powers over this present darkness, against the spiritual forces of evil in the heavenly places. … In all circumstances take up the shield of faith, with which you can extinguish all the flaming darts of the evil one; and take the helmet of salvation, and the sword of the Spirit, which is the word of God, praying at all times in the Spirit, with all prayer and supplication. (Ephesians 6:10–12, 16–18b)

We *need* God's word as we walk through the grief of losing babies in the womb. Even in our sorrow, we mustn't forget the battle that continues in unseen, yet very real, places. In Psalm 119, David writes, "If your law had not been my delight, I would have perished in my affliction" (v. 92). To delight in God's word is the believer's safeguard when a heartbeat isn't detected, when we're still vomiting from morning sickness because our body hasn't recognized our loss yet, or when a friend says something insensitive regarding our baby. The waves of grief caused by miscarriage continue long after those first moments when we learn of our loss. Sadness and confusion can strike many months, even years, later.

Today I searched for my old journal from our years of loss and found this prayer:

Father,

I had so many dreams. I should be eight months pregnant but I also should be nine weeks pregnant. I feel the weight of these "should be's" and my heart is heavy. Everyone has moved on, but reality hits me with newness every day. Dreams of nursery planning, family pictures, baby bumps, and Christmas card announcements. But mostly dreams of knowing my babies, of learning how to be a mom, of watching my husband become a dad. I still bear the mark on my belly that proves my womb was once filled. I hope it stays a while longer. It's one of the only pieces of evidence that my children exist. This is hard. My heart hurts often. I've walked through many storms in this life and God has made me strong through them, but my heart still grieves. It still longs; it still fails. But the trueness of Psalm 119:92 is evident to me:

> If your law had not been my delight,
> I would have perished in my affliction.

Thank you, that you've given me grace to trust your will—even when it hurts. Thank you for the hope found in your Word that I can delight in and cling to. You are my treasure. You are more than enough for me. My heart can be so bitter and hurt. Thank you that you hold me fast. Please help me to bring you glory in this trial. Help me to have grace for others. When everyone else I love forgets my children and my pain I know you always remember. You always care and you're always here. Amen.

We are not left to languish in the gut-wrenching grief of pregnancy loss. God has given us his word, which tells us of his character, and his character reminds us that he is a very present help in our time of need (Psalm 46:1). We always need his word, but we are most aware of it when faced with affliction. We need to treasure it as the gift it is.

## Growing in our Delight

Because I know my own heart, I know there are some of you who might be concerned about your lack of delight in the Scriptures. Maybe reading your Bible is always a challenge for you, but especially when faced with the loss of a baby. You might have loved studying the Bible before, but now it feels impossible. Grief has exhausted your mind.

Whether you are living off the Bible like it is physical bread or you barely think to pick it up, there's room to grow for all of us. If you don't love his word now, you can start seeking to love it more today. Prayer is our first step. We can call out to God, asking him to grow our delight in his word, even in our weary grief. Likewise, we can reach out to friends, mentors, or our husband to pray this over us. Then open his word, dear saint. Open it and listen to how it is pointing you to your suffering Savior, Jesus Christ. See how he kneels down to weep with Mary and Martha over their brother's death (John 11:33–35). Look at how, instead of being frustrated with Mary over her accusation, he is moved by her tears. Watch as the Savior of the world is beaten, spat upon, and hung on a criminal's cross, yet speaks no defense(Luke 22:63; Matthew 27:30, 32–50). He suffered for you (1 Peter 2:21, 3:18). He is the Man of Sorrows, well-acquainted with grief (Isaiah 53:3). He is acquainted with your grief, too.

I found solace in the Psalms during my losses. When I felt like everyone around me was able to easily bear children, I could cry out, "You fill their womb with treasure; they are satisfied with children, and they leave their abundance to their infants. As for me, I shall behold your face in righteousness; when I awake, I shall be satisfied with your likeness." (Psalm 17:14b–15). When my heart ached for God's comfort but I couldn't feel his presence, I lamented, "O my God, I cry by day, but you do not answer, and by night, but I find no rest." (Psalm 22:2).

The Psalms are a wonderful place to start if you aren't sure where to begin. You can read them and use them as guided prayers of lament over your baby to God. Meditate on the truths about God you find there. Ponder his steadfast love. We must always rely on the Holy Spirit to help us. He can reveal to us what a passage is preaching about God's character, provision, and heart for his children. As we read, the Spirit can move us to savor the way God carries his people through suffering like a shepherd carries his wounded sheep. Through the work of the Spirit, we can delight in who God is. How he's gracious, merciful, slow to anger, abounding in steadfast love, good to all, merciful to all, powerful, mighty in his deeds, sovereign, faithful in all his words, and kind in all his works (Psalm 145:8–13). How he upholds those who are falling, raises the humble, provides for our needs, satisfies our desires, hears our cries, saves and preserves us, and is near to those who call on him in truth (Psalm 145:14–20).

Even still, there may be times when the grief of losing your baby fills every crevice of your mind; times when you feel like you're being buried alive in the thick mud of sorrow. Your lungs are filled with dust, making it nearly impossible to raise your voice to God. Maybe you've been reading Scripture, but it just doesn't seem to help. You still feel distant from your Creator; you still wonder if he's really with you. I have felt this way. In times like these, how do we delight in his word?

First of all, we can rest in the Scripture we hear preached from the pulpit every week at church. We can take that word with us throughout our week and meditate on it. After all, for many years, this was how the people of God heard from the Bible. It is only in recent centuries that we have our own copy. When the pain is too heavy, we can also listen to the audio Bible. I found this particularly helpful when I faced sorrow or anxiety brought on by grief over my babies. Another option is to ask our husband or a friend to read Scripture to us. God can use a passage a friend sends us, a verse we heard at church, or even a song or hymn packed with biblical truth to speak to us. We need his word. God knows that. In seasons of grief, when we feel crushed under the loss of our baby, we can trust that God will carry us through and put his word before us.

A couple Sundays after we lost our first baby, I sat in the pew at church fighting back tears. I felt so isolated, so abandoned by God and others. Was God really with me? Did he really care? The answer to my questions first came through a worship song inspired by Psalm 23, then through the sermon preached on Exodus where God leads his people through the Red Sea. And when I arrived home, a package perched on the doorstep holding a devotional on Psalm 23 and a mug that read "He restores my soul" awaited me. Through tears I began to believe that yes, God really was with me. I could no longer doubt his presence.

One of my favorite passages in the Bible is found in Isaiah 55:

> For as the rain and the snow come down from heaven
>     and do not return there but water the earth,
> making it bring forth and sprout,
>     giving seed to the sower and bread to the eater,
> so shall my word be that goes out from my mouth;
>     it shall not return to me empty,
> but it shall accomplish that which I purpose,
>     and shall succeed in the thing for which I sent it. (vv. 10–11)

God's word doesn't return void. It will always accomplish his purpose in our lives and the lives of others. Even when it feels like we aren't being encouraged or changed or even comforted by his word, we can cling to the promise that he is still working through it in unseen ways. This causes our soul to rest in him.

## Taking Hold of the Gift of the Word

In the first chapter of the Gospel of John, we find the mind-blowing truth that Jesus is the Living Word.

> In the beginning was the Word, and the Word was with God, and the Word was God. He was in the beginning with God. All things were made through him, and without him was not any thing made that was made. In him was life, and the life was the light of men. (John 1:1–4)

Ideas like this are too much for our brains to grasp. When we pick up our Bibles and read them or when we hear Scripture preached on a Sunday, Jesus, the Savior of the world, is *speaking*. Not just speaking, but speaking to *us*. Jesus is the Word made flesh who dwelt among us, Immanuel. He is "full of grace and truth" (John 1:14). He's the true manna from heaven; the Bread of Life.

Jesus says, in John 6 when talking to the Israelites, "Truly, truly, I say to you, it was not Moses who gave you the bread from heaven, but my Father gives you the true bread from heaven. For the bread of God is he who comes down from heaven and gives life to the world" (vv. 32–33). He claims to be the very bread of heaven of which he speaks: "I am the bread of life; whoever comes to me shall not hunger, and whoever believes in me shall never thirst" (v. 35). Those who take hold of this Bread as their only hope for salvation will not only find eternal life but also eternal satisfaction which only comes through belief in Jesus Christ (vv. 47, 58).

When Jesus was tempted by Satan in the wilderness, he made a striking statement. After being tempted to provide for himself food to satisfy his great hunger, he responded saying, "It is written, 'Man shall not live by bread alone, but by every word that comes from the mouth of God' " (Matthew 4:4). We live by feasting on the Word of God, the Bread of Life. Maybe you feel up to reading a couple chapters or maybe you can only repeat the phrase "I believe, help my unbelief" for days on repeat. It isn't the amount that matters. It is not our efforts that sustain us, but the food itself: Christ. He can make much out of only a little food (Matthew 14:13–21). He holds us up in our grief; he sustains our faith by the power of his word.

The Bible is a gift for those of us suffering the grief of miscarriage. With Peter, we cry out, "Lord, to whom shall we go? You have the words of eternal life" (John 6:68). Jesus is the Living Word. Let's run to him in our sorrow. We need the Living Word, the Bread of Life, to comfort and carry us through our affliction. Let's take hold and eat.

## Psalm of Lament

O Lord, God of my salvation,
    I cry out day and night before you.
Let my prayer come before you;
    incline your ear to my cry!

For my soul is full of troubles,
    and my life draws near to Sheol.
I am counted among those who go down to the pit;
    I am a man who has no strength,
like one set loose among the dead,
    like the slain that lie in the grave,
like those whom you remember no more,
    for they are cut off from your hand.
You have put me in the depths of the pit,
    in the regions dark and deep.
Your wrath lies heavy upon me,
    and you overwhelm me with all your waves. (Psalm 88:1–7)

## Guided Lament

God, the waves of grief threaten to drown me. Once I feel like I can breathe, another comes crashing over my head. Yet you are sovereign over the waves. I don't know what to do with that fact right now, but I know you're also good. Please have mercy on me. For Jesus's sake. Amen.

## Bring Your Lament to God:

Chapter 8

# The Gift of Loving Your Husband through Loss

## *Lord, Sustain Us*

*I saw red*
*like an alarm,*
*telling the world that something was*
*wrong.*

*I gasped,*
*counted to three:*

*1, 2, 3...*
*then looked.*

*I guess*
*nothing can really prepare you*
*to hold your tiny, still baby*
*inside your hand.*

*It had only been a few hours* since I laid, exposed on a cold table with my nearly empty uterus on the fuzzy screen. The once sunny, humid day had given way to a summer storm. Torrential rain pelted the metal of our car as the silence thickened between my husband and me. I watched the droplets form into puddles as I fought back my own flood of tears. We picked up takeout as we often did, but this day was far from normal. We were entering a new normal. Life without our baby. Life after loss.

I continued to experience severe cramping for four days. During one trip to the bathroom, my legs faltered as contractions that had slowed suddenly intensified. Unsure of what was happening, I sat back down. Sudden pressure, then relief. With pounding in my chest and tightly closed eyes, I sat in a moment of shock and fear. Gripping the counter to steady myself, I slowly opened my eyes and peered into the porcelain toilet, taking in all that was left of my child.

Miscarriage is confusing, isn't it? Many women experience earth-shattering moments like this and feel unsure of what to do next. One woman shared with me how she birthed her tiny baby in a restaurant bathroom and sat back down at dinner in disbelief. The utter shock of realities we face in miscarriage leave us stunned. I wasn't sure what to do with what I saw. In those days of raw grief, I decided to hold what was left of my precious baby. Every molecule of my body longed to be near to this tiny person who, until a couple of days before, was growing within me—my baby, born too soon. And I had a choice. I could either bear the gravity of those moments alone, or I could reach out to my husband to bear it with me.

My struggle with this choice was that words he had spoken days before left me feeling isolated and misunderstood. Though I can't remember his exact comment today, I remember the feelings I felt when I heard it. While our baby still passed from my body, he feared depression was pulling me down like a whirlpool drains water. But in trying to help me, he actually made me feel like I should *hide* my grief from him.

Yet, I knew if I didn't invite him into this moment, I might regret my decision forever. I sent him a text, asking if he wanted to see what I was seeing. He came into the bathroom and we searched for our baby together. There, in all the ugliness of miscarriage, a marriage was strengthened. The space we'd let grow between us in the matter of just a few days began to close up.

## Miscarriage Puts Pressure on a Marriage

Pregnancy loss can feel like placing your marriage in a pressure cooker. Maybe your husband hasn't done a good job of trying to understand your grief. Maybe he has seemed bothered by your tears or impatient at the time it is taking you to heal. Because of this, some women feel as if they must hide the grief of losing their baby from the very person they sleep next to each night. But the truth is, your husband is grieving too.

I admit that I sometimes treated our miscarriages as if they were something that was happening to me rather than to *us*. As a mother, we long for and miss our baby. It's easy to be overcome by our own sense of loss and forget that our husband lost his baby as well. Some women might be tempted to compare degrees and levels of grief. *He didn't experience losing the child that was growing within his very body* or *He didn't have to go through the trauma I've lived through, or the physical pain of miscarriage.* These things are true and deeply gut-wrenching realities we face when we lose a baby. It's helpful to remember that our husbands are grieving in their own way too. The key is to remember that miscarriage is a shared loss, and neither of you have to grieve on your own.

Many couples report their marriage was made stronger through losing a baby. Sadly, some who faced ongoing years of infertility or recurrent miscarriage felt these painful trials chipped away slowly at the sweetness of their union. Miscarriage and infertility can make intimacy in a marriage extremely difficult. Sometimes fear of more losses can cause a couple to struggle; other times we can become tempted to dwindle intimacy down to the mere act of trying to achieve pregnancy. Opportunities to lash out at each other seem to lurk around every corner when we're hurting (ask me how I know). Bitterness and resentment can take root as quickly as a thorny weed in a flower garden, stealing nutrients away from a healthy marriage. The strong bond of a marriage can be weakened by resentment, hurt, unforgiveness, and harsh words. Couples walking through pregnancy loss must have their guard up, not against each other, but against Satan's attacks. Just as our spouse may hurt us, we have the potential to hurt them with our words and actions as we walk through this grief. Both men and women can learn to love their spouse even as they walk through this incredible loss.

## Understanding His Grief

Every marriage is unique. Because of this, it would be impossible to address every single scenario or struggle a couple might face as they experience miscarriage. If you have been deeply hurt by your husband's handling of your grief, I'm so sorry. I encourage you to seek marital counseling together from your pastor, a trusted therapist, or a mentor. May God bring healing to your heart and to your marriage.

Generally, our husbands will face the grief of losing an unborn child differently than us. Because they didn't carry our baby within their own body, they may not feel the same level of attachment as we do. When my husband and I lost our first baby, this difference bothered me. I wondered why he didn't seem to grieve as deeply as I was. It's helpful to remember that while mothers have an immediate, scientifically proven bond to their child from the moment of conception, fathers bond with their baby as they take care of them once they are born. It makes sense that, though they are sad, they haven't had the chance to bond with our baby as we have. This is especially true in the majority of miscarriages where the baby is still too small for the father to feel their kicks. That fact—that they didn't experience the closeness we felt when we carried our baby—could produce its own layer of grief. We felt the evidence of their lives as our hormones made us queasy and our bodies began shifting to make room for them. Yet though their grief takes on a different form, they still grieve. Many men experience feelings of confusion, sorrow, anger, and fear as they walk through this loss.

It was not until months after our third baby left us that my husband opened up to me about his own grief. He shared how he would drive to work and lament to God over our suffering. He asked God if it was something he had done—some unknown sin in his life—that caused the death of our babies. He was hurting. He was wrestling with God and I was oblivious.

This is a common response to miscarriage among men. They worry that they are not worthy of a child. Some struggle with feelings of betrayal or fear that God is punishing them. And many of them don't share these feelings with their wife until later, if ever. This means our husbands are grieving, even if they don't show it.

As wives, we can seek to understand their grief and draw them out. We can let them know that we are a safe space for them to share by not comparing our grief to theirs. Husbands and wives both must respect and love each other through the painful loss of their baby. We can do this by God's grace and with the help of the Holy Spirit.

## Understanding His Point of View

One of the hardest things for me during our losses was how often my husband had to leave me to go to work as I was miscarrying. I felt angry, hurt, and incredibly alone. Most men are obligated to go to work when their wife miscarries. They want to comfort their wife, but they *can't* lose their job. Incredible pressure and shame are placed on their backs from all sides. When I recognized this, it became easier to be understanding toward my husband. When walking the path of pregnancy loss, it's helpful to remember our husbands have different priorities, obligations, and perspectives than us—many of which leave them feeling ill-equipped and like they're failing.

Let's put ourselves in their shoes for just a moment. For most husbands, their top priority is to support their wife in her grief. They seek to help her physically as she labors. Some men even witness their wives experiencing life-threatening circumstances, which can be terrifying. They are concerned for her physical healing. Many men watch their wife's tears and feel completely at a loss of how to help her. They are fixers, and they can't fix grief. It's not in their power to bring back their baby and make everything right again, and they hate it. Husbands who love the Lord want to love their wives well through loss, coming alongside them physically, spiritually, and emotionally. Yet so many don't feel confident in how to do so.

Upon writing this chapter, I recalled those early moments of grief to my husband when his words had wounded me. Neither of us remember his exact words, but he does remember his feelings of uncertainty and how he just didn't know what to say. This is often the case when our husband's words wound us in the throes of miscarriage. As wives, we can love our husbands through loss by giving them grace when they make mistakes or don't handle our grief in the way we hoped. After all, we will likely hurt them and need their grace, too.

Our husbands have a lot on their shoulders. When we take these different priorities and obligations into consideration, it helps us understand our husband's point of view, which in turn helps us to love him well, as he is seeking to love us.

## Miscarriage and Intimacy

A couple weeks after losing our first child, the doctor gave us permission to begin trying again. According to her, I was physically healed and ready to bear a child. The near-empty tissue box on my nightstand, however, was a testament to my emotional state. I missed my baby, and intimacy with my husband was a reminder of this great void. I couldn't separate the act of sex from the truth that God used our bodies to create a baby, and that baby was now gone. I was also terrified of getting pregnant again and then losing another baby. Sadly, I did lose more. I was surprised to find that each loss affected our intimacy differently. There's no denying that miscarriage has a huge impact on a husband and wife's sex life. There are so many factors that play into the differing experience each couple may have. Hormones, marital health, trauma, physical healing, having other children, and more all influence our feelings toward sex after miscarriage.

The desire for sex after experiencing a miscarriage can range from non-existent to persistent. Some women feel shame regarding enjoying making love to their spouse following a miscarriage because they fear it means they have forgotten their baby. They worry that the feelings of joy and ecstasy ushered in during sex with their husband might mean they aren't as sad over their baby as they thought. This can bring about feelings of undue guilt and shame.

Hormones play a huge role here. Sometimes in our grief, what we long for most is to be near to our husband. No shame should be felt for that. It is a beautiful, holy thing when a husband and wife who are grieving come together as one. We're reminded again that joy and sorrow can intertwine.

Yet, for many women, the thought of sex only reminds them of their baby. This can be incredibly hard on the couple. Women might also be fearful of becoming pregnant again when their heart isn't quite ready. Husbands must be gentle with their wife, giving her time to heal both physically and emotionally. Eventually, the two must come back together, but patience is required on both sides. Husbands and wives should seek to prefer the other as they walk through the loss of their baby. This is a key way we learn to love our spouse through grief.

## To Women Who Have Been Hurt

Over the years, as women have shared their experiences with me, I have been appalled at the responses I've seen some Christian husbands have toward their wife's grief, from statements that devalue the life of their own child to hurtful comments about their wife's sorrow. If you have been harmed by your husband's ignorance,

I'm so sorry. It shouldn't be this way. God sees your pain, and he cares how you are treated. Sometimes learning to love our husband through loss looks like pursuing counseling and confronting these things in love. Other times it may mean we have to choose to overlook and cover his offenses with grace. This is hard. But it is possible with the help of the Holy Spirit.

Certainly, for any couple walking through loss, whether we have a healthy marriage or not, there will be times where we hurt each other with our words or actions. Putting off bitterness and working through these hurts together is a huge part of loving our spouse even as we face the grief of miscarriage. As we walk this painful road together, hand in hand, we grow in patience, graciousness, humble servitude, and love. And through the power of the Holy Spirit, we can come out on the other side stronger together than ever.

I believe this is possible where you have two people—man and woman—committed to loving each other through the grief miscarriage brings. However, I am not naïve to the reality that sometimes one spouse is unwilling to forgive offenses, repent when necessary, or grow in love. Maybe you have gone to war for your marriage and feel like you are standing on the battlefield alone, sword in hand, ready to fight. But your husband is sleeping soundly in his bed unaware, or worse, *uncaring* about the battle at hand. I can imagine the sting you feel in your heart.

Keep praying; keep fighting. Do not lose hope that God can wake your spouse up and restore the beauty of your marriage. But more than that, you can hope in Christ. You may feel alone, but

God is always with you. He never leaves your side and is holding up your weary arms in the fight.

Heartbreakingly, we know that some marriages end in divorce and sometimes grief plays a part. If that's your story, I'm so sorry. I'm sorry for the brokenness of this world and the pain you must feel. I pray that you will know that you can run to God with your sorrow and lay your lament at his feet. He will sustain your faith.

## Sustain Us, God

When I look back at our years of miscarriage, I see how God sustained us through that time. He alone deserves the credit for every moment we asked for forgiveness or drew near to each other instead of hiding.

God is the sustainer of all things. He's sustaining the very breath in your lungs as you read this sentence, and he has the power to sustain your marriage. He can heal what is broken, bring repentance where it's necessary, and revive the joy you once had together. If you aren't sure where to start, *pray*. Pray to this God who can bind up every wound. The God who brings dead things to life. Sustain our marriages through loss, Lord. We need you.

## Psalm of Lament

Hear my prayer, O LORD;
let my cry come to you!
Do not hide your face from me
    in the day of my distress!

Incline your ear to me;
    answer me speedily in the day when I call!

For my days pass away like smoke,
    and my bones burn like a furnace.
My heart is struck down like grass and has withered;
    I forget to eat my bread.
Because of my loud groaning
    my bones cling to my flesh.
I am like a desert owl of the wilderness,
    like an owl of the waste places;
I lie awake;
    I am like a lonely sparrow on the housetop.
    (Psalm 102:1–11)

## Guided Lament

Father, sometimes it feels like you don't hear me, or maybe you don't care. I'm begging you to answer me, to comfort me, to sit with me in the grief of my baby. Draw near to me, God. I need you. For Jesus's sake. Amen.

## Bring Your Lament to God:

# Chapter 9

# The Gift of Growing in Grace

## *Lord, Their Words Left Wounds*

*When the ER doctor came in,*
*she asked "How many is this?"*
*and I told her, "Three."*
*"Three children?" she asked.*
*"Yes," I said. But still,*
*she kept looking at me.*
*"Any living children?"*
*she asked. It must have been*
*a box she needed to check.*
*"Oh," I said,*
*adjusting my mask,*
*"No," I said,*
*understanding what*
*she had asked.*

*And I listened to the sound*
*her pen made as she*
*scratched out my answer.*
—Rachel Joy Welcher[24]

*I sat in a frigid leather chair*, anxiety pulsing through every limb. I braced myself for what was to come, nervously glancing at my husband who was sitting beside me. This wasn't our first meeting. We had met with these two spiritual leaders before, and each meeting seemed to grow in intensity. His harsh words sent a shock so deep within my soul, I thought my body might crumble:

"You're too downcast ... you were too downcast during your miscarriages."

He added: "Others have suffered more than you and handled it better."

To this day, I'm not sure this man has a clue how deeply those words have marked my soul. A woman has three babies slip silently from her womb, leaving her body feeling empty and her heart shattered, and this is what is said to her ... by a man who was supposed to shepherd her? This is my own story of wounding words. It's not the only story that occurred during the loss of my babies, just the worst one. This is the memory that still hurts and haunts, years later.

Words can wound, especially when aimed at the grieving. Maybe you have experienced these words—the ones that make your body grow numb with deepening sorrow. The minute they enter your heart, they pierce, flip flop your stomach, and send electricity to your feet, making you want to run away. You want to scream, sprint, sob, and shake someone all at once. The words reinforce the lie that you are alone and misunderstood in your pain. The isolation can wrap itself around you like an unexpected fog. And what's worse is that, for many of us, these immensely hurtful words come from the mouths of fellow believers. Christians are called to bear each other's burdens, but sometimes it feels like they simply *add* to them.

How should we respond to these wounding words, these experiences that shake and shape us? Should we address wrong thinking and hurtful phrases directly, or let them slide? How on earth do we find grace to cover distressing words and heal the ways they leave us broken? Is there any fruit born from wounding words? We'll get to all of these questions in this chapter.

First things first, let's address some common phrases spoken to parents, specifically mothers, who are walking through pregnancy loss.

## Please Stop Saying That

At least ... it was early.

At least ... you have other children.

At least ... you know you can get pregnant.

At least ... you can adopt.

Whatever the *at least* entails, it's almost never helpful and usually deeply hurtful. In saying *at least*, we not only diminish the pain of losing a pre-born child, but we also devalue the life of the unborn. When Christians—who make up the majority of the pro-life movement—say this, it begs the question: do we truly believe that babies in the womb have value? Are we really as pro-life as we claim? These dismissals also stem from a type of stoicism that has no place in the body of Christ. It's like saying, "Look on the bright side, the death of your baby isn't so bad. It could be worse. They aren't worth grieving." That's pretty ugly, isn't it? Of course it could be worse, but goodness, it could be better, too. Our babies could be here, alive in our arms. These types of sentiments shouldn't reside in the minds and mouths of Christians.

*You'll have another baby.*

When I lost my first baby at nine weeks, it was as if there was a gaping black hole in my stomach where my child once resided. The impact of never holding that baby left my arms heavy with longing. One of my well-meaning midwives at the time tried to encourage me with this sentiment. She was right. I did have more babies—two more—and all of them passed away before their little bodies could be placed on my chest. There are a couple reasons we should stop saying this to grieving mamas. First of all, it's like telling a person whose husband is dying that "Hey, you can always marry again." We would never do this. So why do we think it's okay when speaking about an unborn child? We aren't *almost* parents; we became mothers at the moment our baby was conceived.

There is no way we can know or promise that anyone *will* have another baby. Many women go on to have miscarriage after miscarriage, never getting to experience the joy of parenting one of their little ones. Others struggle with long-term infertility after experiencing miscarriage. We can never know what a woman's motherhood journey will look like. For many, it may only include loss. Furthermore, we don't want another baby; we wanted *that* baby. The one we felt our bodies begin to shift for. The one that had made us nauseous and fatigued for weeks. Their presence was obvious to us, though unknown to those around us. Yet, that didn't make our baby any less valuable because *babies don't replace babies.* Every child conceived, no matter the length of life, bears the image of the Almighty God, uniquely created to bring him glory.

*Maybe God was protecting you*
*from a baby with special needs.*

This might be the most heartbreaking thing a person could say to women who have miscarried. This, too, reveals a heart that doesn't truly value every single life. Our pro-abortion culture advocates for the brutal murder of unborn babies with disabilities. They declare that a life of disability is not a life worth living. Christians, of all people, should reject this notion. Every life God creates is inherently valuable; formed in the *imago Dei*. When Christians declare the death of a precious baby as God's protection, we don't look much different than the pro-abortionist marching with a sign in the Women's March. Is it better that a mother and father would lose their baby rather than getting to know and kiss and raise their child with disabilities?

*Do you think it was the _____ (coffee, exercise, stress)?*

This kind of question is so common and only adds shame to an already stinging wound. Questions like these place the blame in the mother's lap, and if comments like this have been directed at you, I am so sorry. Your miscarriages are not a result of your diet or exercise routine or the amount of stress on your shoulders. Miscarriage *can* happen due to ingesting harmful substances, but for most women, this simply isn't the case. One in four pregnancies end in miscarriage, and the cause very rarely has anything to do with something the mother has ingested or a choice she has made.

*Remember the 12-week rule.*
*You might have a miscarriage.*

The 12-week rule says a woman should wait to share about her pregnancy until she reaches twelve weeks gestation, the point when miscarriage becomes less likely. The decision of whether or not to share a pregnancy before twelve weeks is deeply personal and there isn't one right choice. While it may be helpful for some women to wait, we have made it a rule for *every* woman to follow. What started as advice to spare women grief ends up causing many women to feel isolated in their pain. They feel they can't share about their baby's loss because they didn't share about their life. They were told it would be easier this way, but is it? Is it easier to know great loss, yet hide it from everyone around you? Certainly, some women are relieved that they don't have to publicly pronounce the loss of their baby, and that's okay. But for many, hiding their grief only increases their sorrow.

Personally, I share about my babies pretty early. I lost count of the times other women warned me to not share. Just like some believe a baby in the first trimester should be kept secret, they also believe miscarriage to be sacred—something to be grieved privately. They may even claim that sharing puts people in an awkward place, forcing them to acknowledge our loss. What would it look like to unbelievers if instead of encouraging secrecy, more Christians rejoiced in a woman's decision to share about the youngest of lives in the womb? Would it send out reminders into our dark world that unborn babies—even those younger than 12 weeks—are indeed worth rejoicing and grieving over?

### *Saying nothing.*

Many times, what hurts more than any harsh words or careless dismissals are the words left *unspoken*. A friend or family member simply says nothing at the news of our loss. Maybe you've even had people seemingly avoid you. They dodge eye contact at church and slip past you, making you feel as if your grief is causing *them* discomfort. They have forfeited entering your sorrow and bearing your burden because it's just too much or they don't know what to say. In most cases, these friends desperately don't want to say the wrong thing and further our grief. Yet the silence can be deafening. Christians must learn how to engage with those who are walking through miscarriage in a biblical way, coming alongside them and weeping with them. We don't have to say the perfect thing, but a simple "I'm so sorry for the loss of your baby. Can I bring you a meal and sit with you?" goes a very long way.

## Truths that Can Harm

Often, when someone close to us (and sometimes even those who aren't close to us) is confronted with our loss, they may feel the need to "speak truth" to us. They might tell us to trust that God is working all things for our good (Romans 8:28). Maybe our laments don't sound very theologically correct, and people jump to rebuke us instead of giving us grace. True words spoken at the wrong time can stir up pain like a dust storm.

As Christians who stand on the word of God, we are often tempted to assume that because what we're saying is true, it can't possibly be wrong to say it. Any recipient of our words should be able to handle them. Furthermore, we might even believe that we've paid our dues—surely, they should feel better now that we've reminded them God is sovereign. Problem solved. Many Christians trade in the work of bearing burdens for a passage on suffering, assuming that is all a sufferer needs. They can move on now. But is that what it means when Scripture says to "weep with those who weep" (Romans 12:15)?

The grief of miscarriage isn't wiped away with Bible verses. It is not a tidy grief or one easily overcome by platitudes. True words carelessly spoken are like covering an infected wound with gauze and expecting it to heal. Learning to live without the babies we love takes time and tender care from God and those around us. There is no right amount of time. Just as with most tears we cry during our time on this earth, the tears of miscarriage will be wiped away only by Christ in glory (Revelation 21:4).

It's certainly true that we can trust God—Romans 8:28 still stands—but if these truths are used to quiet the desperate cries of a mother who is grieving her unborn child, they only cause harm. Women who are walking through this terrible suffering do need to be reminded of God's goodness, that he can be trusted, and that his plans are best. These truths matter, but how and when we say them also matters.

Instead of having Christian platitudes on the tip of our tongue, believers in Christ can learn to truly listen. We must wait upon the Lord as we converse with women walking through this often long-term season of suffering. We must learn forbearance. Even Job's friends, who sat in complete silence for seven days and nights before opening their mouths, were still rebuked by God for much of what they said (Job 2:13). Many Christians in our Western culture barely let someone state their feelings before offering up "But God is good. Rejoice always!" What if instead, prayer and patience led us through every sentence and response? What if we asked the Holy Spirit to help us discern when to speak and when to remain quiet, when to share truth and when to let it pass? Proverbs 25:11 says, "A word fitly spoken is like apples of gold in a setting of silver." I had no idea what this meant when I first read it. I eventually came to a similar conclusion as the one I found on the website, *Got Questions*:

> "The 'apples of gold in a setting of silver' seem to refer to exquisitely crafted ornamental jewelry or artwork. The language evokes a design that has been etched, sculpted, or engraved in silver, like filigree. This interpretation supports the idea that well-spoken words have attractive and valuable qualities because skill and artistry have gone into fashioning them."[25]

A timely word (or truth) stands out, makes an impact. It's sweet to the hearer's ears and skillfully contrived. We find a similar thought in Proverbs 15: "To make an apt answer is a joy to a man, and a word in season, how good it is!" (Proverbs 15:23) If we want to be an encouragement to our friends and family who have lost babies, we must take these verses to heart. The Holy Spirit will lead us as we do.

## What To Do with Wounding Words

Most of you have experienced words like the ones I describe in this chapter. Maybe some of you can still feel the weight of them, even now. What do we do when someone's words leave us with incredible hurt and frustration?

When met with these types of comments, we have two options: ignore or confront. We can try our best to let the words dissipate; to forget them. Or, if we can't forget, we can lovingly confront the person about why what they said was hurtful or unhelpful. Either option is justified.

I've always struggled to know how to respond when someone asks me how many children I have. The truthful answer, as I type this today, is either five or six. It was suspected but couldn't be confirmed that my first pregnancy was a set of twins. Based on my symptoms, my midwives believed I may have lost one twin around six weeks, experiencing vanishing twin syndrome, and then went on to lose the other at nine weeks. I will always wonder if I actually have four babies waiting for me in heaven. Regardless, when I was pregnant with my second earth side son, William, a doctor asked this question which is so complicated for those of us who've lost babies to answer. I fumbled over my words saying, *Well ... I ... I have one living child and three I lost to miscarriage. And I'm pregnant with our fi—*

"So you have one child." She cut me off.

I was baffled—completely unable to speak. Even years after my losses I felt the sting of her words that sought to minimize my grief. In one fell swoop she had devalued the lives of all my unborn babies. I didn't have the emotional energy that day to attempt to make this doctor understand how her words hurt me. Have you had experiences like this? Things were said and feelings were hurt, but you simply chose to overlook and pour grace on people's words for your own sanity. You have the freedom to do this. You don't have to correct every single untruth spoken to you. Sometimes, we have to let things go, remembering the Holy Spirit does the work of convicting and reforming others. If you are anything like me though, you might *want* to confront them instead. How do we do that graciously?

Firstly, we must seek to correct these harmful words with a motive that is less about our hurt and more about coming alongside the person who said it. We want them to understand how to glorify God by refining their speech and becoming comforters to those who are suffering miscarriage, rather than a hindrance to their healing. In all of this, we must speak the truth in love (Ephesians 4:15). And lastly, we must leave the work of conviction to the Holy Spirit. Usually, fellow believers (and also non-believers) don't realize how their words have hurt us. Most will respond with sadness and repentance. This is great! But if not, we can choose to forgive them in our hearts, letting go of any bitterness we might be harboring.

Whether we silently overlook or gently correct, we should be gracious in our response. All who walk the earth (aside from Jesus of course) have said hurtful things. We must be ready and willing to forgive others as we have been forgiven (Ephesians 4:32). Ultimately, our healing comes from God above, not from whether we receive the apology we hope for. Don't place your healing in the hands of any person.

## God, Our Healer

At the beginning of this chapter, I asked what we do with words that wound us. Ultimately, no amount of perfectly crafted encouragement from friends, family, and acquaintances will bring us the healing we so long for. Even if we don't experience any hurtful comments throughout all of our losses, we will still need the healing only God can usher into our hearts. We are given the great joy and privilege to run to God in our hurt. We are free to lament to him about the phrases spoken to us, over us, and about us. He sees, he hears, he knows, and he *cares*.

In Exodus 3:7–8, we see God's care for his people:

> Then the Lord said, "I have surely *seen* the affliction of my people who are in Egypt and have *heard* their cry because of their taskmasters. I *know* their sufferings, and *I have come down to deliver them* out of the hand of the Egyptians and to bring them up out of that land to a good and broad land, a land flowing with milk and honey. (emphasis added)

God saw the affliction of his people, he heard their cry, he knew their sufferings, and he came down to deliver them. Likewise, God sees how the words of other people have hurt you. He knows what was said and why it was wrong. He hears your cries and your prayers of lament. And he cares for your heart and soul. As he acted with the Israelites, he will act in your situation too, even if only to comfort your broken heart. For we know he is ever near to the broken-hearted (Psalm 34:18).

## The Gifts Within Words that Wound Us

Truly, there is fruit that grows, despite wounding words. This doesn't excuse the thoughtlessness of others, but it does mean that our good God brings about good gifts in spite of the hurtful things said to those experiencing miscarriage.

One way we can allow God to bring about good from the bad is through his work in our own hearts as we learn to pour grace out on others while we seek to occasionally overlook offenses or graciously correct them. We often wish for grace from others in our suffering. But truly, women and men walking through miscarriage will need to give lots of grace to those who fumble over their losses. Through pregnancy loss, we can cultivate hearts that offer grace to others and seek to cover offenses (Proverbs 10:12; 1 Peter 4:8).

When "at least you can get pregnant" is thrown our way, we can kindly explain that while it is a blessing to conceive, we lost actual babies. Comparing losing our children to infertility is unfair to both miscarriage mamas and women who long to be mamas. And we grow in grace as we seek to come alongside them, helping them understand and equipping them with a better response. When someone shrugs and asks "why don't you just adopt?", we can remind them that adoption is not as easy as they may assume—there is a lot of heartache involved in adoption too, and we aren't promised babies via that route either. Again, we grow in grace as we gently encourage them to think rightly about these things so that they don't continue to hurt others. Growing in grace might also look like reaching out to that friend who seems distant after losing your babies (though, you certainly don't have to). It might mean assuming the best of her—that she most likely wants to help you but feels ill-equipped to do so. Growing in grace is a gift that will look different for each individual.

We grow in grace in other ways too. When we suffer through the sorrow wrought by hurtful words, we gain a deeper understanding and an indispensable perspective of those who are walking through various types of suffering. We learn specifically how *not* to address women or couples who are withstanding the grief of miscarriage. But also, we become better equipped in our response to those who are suffering other types of loss. One beautiful truth (that we will dig into more in another chapter) is that God uses our suffering for the good of others. The God of comfort fills our hearts with his comfort, and we pour out that comfort on those around us who need it.

> Blessed be the God and Father of our Lord Jesus Christ, the Father of mercies and God of all comfort, who comforts us in all our affliction, so that we may be able to comfort those who are in any affliction, with the comfort with which we ourselves are comforted by God. (2 Corinthians 1:3–4)

This is the good fruit yielded from hurtful words. We know how to comfort those who experience the careless words of others with the comfort we have received from Christ.

More than anything, words that wound cause us to run to God, and in doing so we find the warm embrace and comfort of our

Father. He sees, he hears, he knows, and he *cares*. He is acting on your behalf even now.

## Psalm of Lament

> O Lord, all my longing is before you;
> my sighing is not hidden from you.
> My heart throbs; my strength fails me,
> and the light of my eyes—it also has gone from me.
> My friends and companions stand aloof from my plague,
> and my nearest kin stand far off. (Psalm 38:9–11)

## Guided Lament

Lord, it feels like everyone is moving on while I'm standing still. They've forgotten me; they've forgotten my baby. I feel so utterly alone. Where are you, God? Amen.

## Bring Your Lament to God:

## Chapter 10

# The Gift of the Church

### *Lord, Bless the Burden Bearers*

*Abide with me: fast falls the eventide;*
*the darkness deepens; Lord, with me abide.*
*When other helpers fail and comforts flee,*
*Help of the helpless, O abide with me.*
—"Abide with Me" by Henry Francis Lyte

*I lay on the couch* wrapped in a blanket and my own numbness as my husband kissed my forehead. I watched him close the door with loneliness slithering around my heart like a snake coils around its prey, suffocating it. For weeks, I had been feeling my pregnancy symptoms fade. The nausea came and went. The extreme fatigue had fled. The soreness of my breasts had dissipated. Until finally, my body gave up my baby on my husband's birthday, and then he left for work.

He didn't want to go to work; his job was just so demanding. This was a consistent point of struggle for me as we lost our babies. He often had to leave when I needed him most. Yet God provided through his people.

As I was losing our first child, a friend drove me to an appointment to confirm what was happening. The nightmare intensified. The pain from an internal ultrasound while my uterus contracted left me in a state of severe anxiety, making my whole body shake in torment. But it wasn't a nightmare; it was trauma. My husband couldn't be there, but God was with me through my friend. She was Christ to me.

The night I lost our second baby, two of my closest friends came to sit with me. They brought Panera Bread for dinner and we watched Poldark. They prayed with me, cried with me, and listened as I talked about my fears of the future and how I just wanted my babies. These women were Christ to me.

My two mentors regularly checked on me, brought homemade soups, and prayed for me. While others began to back away, they pressed in. They were Christ to me.

The morning I began to lose our third unborn baby, my husband had to work. My sweet mother came over and sat with me until he came home. She washed my dishes and cleaned my kitchen, brought me medicine and water, prayed over me, and held me. She was Christ to me.

I could go on about how God's people came alongside us in our losses, providing presence and, through it, the comfort of Jesus.

God uses his church, the body of Christ, as his hands and feet to bear the burdens of his saints. Yet, many of us feel isolated as we face the loss of our baby. How do we reconcile the gift of the church with the hurt the people who make up the church can cause?

## Called to Burden-Bearing

Every single person who has trusted in Christ alone to save them from their sin together make up the body of Christ. We are the universal church. Jesus is our head, and we are his hands and feet. Colossians 1:18 says, "he is the head of the body, the church." We find in 1 Corinthians 12 that we "are the body of Christ and individually members of it" (v. 27). Every Christ-follower is a part of the body, and we *need* each other (v. 21).

As the church, we are called to many things, including seeking the lost, providing for the needy, and praying for the saints. We build each other up in love by lovingly speaking the truth (Ephesians 4:15–16). The Spirit gives varying gifts to each person which aid us in living out these callings (1 Corinthians 12:4–11). We rejoice together, and we suffer together (1 Corinthians 12:26; Romans 12:15). We are called to the painful and beautiful work of bearing the burdens of our fellow believers (Galatians 6:2). This certainly includes burdens such as miscarriage. When the church takes burden-bearing seriously, we show we love each other. The love of the saints points to God, who is love (1 John 4:8). As the body functions properly, we display Christ to the world around us. The old hymn reminds us, "And they'll know we are Christians by our love, by our love. Yes, they'll know we are Christians by our love."

When we humble ourselves to serve others in their grief, we look like our Savior who left heaven, took on flesh, and knelt down to live among the grieving and the needy (Philippians 2:8). As we weep with the couple who weeps over their baby, we point to the one who wept (John 11:35). This is why it is so painful when Christians don't seek to bear burdens like miscarriage alongside their fellow saints. We might be tempted to think that if God's people, who have his Spirit, don't care about the loss of our unborn baby, maybe he doesn't either.

Couples who have lost their baby to miscarriage need other saints to bear their burdens with them. They need the church to be the hands and feet of Jesus, lifting them up and carrying their grief alongside them. Though Christians from other churches or even across the world can be an encouragement to us in the grief of baby loss, God often works through our local body. If you are not part of a church near you, I encourage you to find one. Engaging in and receiving from the local church is vital to the faith of a believer, especially when facing the grief of miscarriage.

It is equally vital that, as the body of Christ, we seek to weep with those who are weeping, kneeling down to pick up their burdens, and placing them on our shoulders as if they were our own. The church can bear burdens by bringing meals, weeping alongside the bereaved, lamenting on their behalf, interceding for them in prayer, checking on grieving couples, remembering their baby, and so much more.

But what about when our church doesn't meet our expectations? What if they don't seem to acknowledge the loss of our baby? What if they refuse to bear our burdens?

## Who Will Weep with Me?

While some churches are wonderful at bearing the burdens of those who are suffering miscarriage, others cause harm. Most churches are eager to celebrate new life by providing meals and other acts of services after a woman gives birth. But when a baby dies through miscarriage, meal trains are rarely set in place. Churches are often more comfortable rejoicing with those who rejoice than they are at weeping with those who weep. This must change.

Soon after losing my first baby, I stood in the church foyer chatting with an acquaintance. Her new little one sat nestled in an infant bucket-seat at her feet. A mutual friend came up and showered the other woman with congratulations. This was, of course, completely okay! But afterward, she wholly ignored my grief. She didn't ask how I was doing or seek out how I was feeling. The woman with a baby in her arms received elated rejoicing. But for me, the woman who had lost a baby—*silence*.

Many of us have felt the sting of this silence. Sometimes it continues as certain friendships show their shallow roots, bringing more grief into our lives. The hard truth is that some people aren't willing to bear our burdens. Sometimes, those people surprise you.

Salty tears well up in the eyes of women who have lost a baby and cry out "who will weep with me?" The silence of their church responds, "not us." To know that the people in your church are called to bear your burden and then to witness their refusal to do so can deeply harm your faith.

This is a very real hurt. Yet at the same time, we must remember that it's not possible for every single person in our church to comfort us in our suffering. We shouldn't expect more from other believers than they can give. Walking through the grief of miscarriage often exposes who our steady friends are; it shows us who is eager to carry our grief like the Bible commands. Sadly, it's not uncommon for relationships to dwindle away under the weight of suffering a miscarriage. This can be utterly heart-shattering to a woman grappling with the loss of her baby.

## Those Who Weep

It can be tempting to focus on the hurt caused when people we love keep us at a distance as we grieve. You begin to feel like no one wants to talk to you because they are afraid they will catch your sadness like a contagion. This feeling especially plagues women suffering from recurrent loss or infertility. As I kept losing baby after baby, I often sensed that people did not know what to do with me and my grief. If you have felt this way too, we are not alone. King David felt abandoned by his closest friends in his suffering: "My friends and companions stand aloof from my plague, and my nearest kin stand far off." (Psalm 38:11). As a culture, we can become increasingly uncomfortable as affliction continues. When suffering lingers long, friends do not.

But some friends *do*. And those friends are a revitalizing gift from God. Some friends refuse to let the awkwardness of suffering get in the way of loving us. They are the ones who are willing to weep, pray, encourage, provide, and lament. The ones who seek us, listen to our pain, remember our wounds. They are the burden-bearers in our lives. Friends like that are a deep encouragement to our souls, a reminder that God sees us. Like God used Moses to provide water from a rock, he uses these believers to bring us to the fountain of Living Water, that we might be refreshed in Christ (Exodus 17:6; John 7:37–38). They are his hands and his feet, and they act like it.

If we focus on the Christians who abandon us or who stand far off from our grief, we might be tempted to believe that God has abandoned us. But if we shift our focus to the friends who stay close, we're pointed to the God who draws near. We're reminded of our Savior who weeps with us. Jesus himself knows what it feels like to be isolated. He wept in the garden of Gethsemane hours before his arrest while his closest friends couldn't stay awake to pray for him (Matthew 26:36–46). He called out, "my soul is very sorrowful!" and they fell asleep. But the Father was with him. And Jesus is with us. Even as close as our very soul where his Spirit resides, comforting us.

Truthfully, many people want to help those suffering miscarriage; they just don't know how. Sometimes, in order for others to know how to draw near to us, we need to be willing to ask for help.

## Asking for Help

Some couples experiencing pregnancy loss forfeit the help they could receive from believers in their church by remaining quiet about their loss. This is, of course, a personal choice. There is no rule that claims we must open up to others about our miscarriage. Here's what makes this tricky: when we don't share about our grief, we miss out on the comfort, encouragement, and help that other Christians could provide. We relinquish the beauty of watching God work through his people to strengthen our faith. Opportunities for deeper community and fellowship with other believers fall by the wayside.

If I had hidden my grief, I would have missed out on new and deepened friendships. There are many times I stood in awe of God as he ministered to me through his people that would not be part of my story had I kept quiet. We *need* the church. The church is a gift. No Christian can thrive without it; Scripture is clear on this fact (1 Corinthians 12:12–27; Hebrews 10:25). Simply attending a service in a building every week isn't true fellowship. Biblical fellowship happens when we reach out to serve and allow others to serve us. Other believers don't know how to help us unless we open up about our grief to trusted friends and ask for help. If we are unwilling to do this, we cannot expect our church family to come alongside us.

I fear some women might feel that miscarriage isn't a grief worthy of notifying their church. Maybe you feel it would be bothersome to ask others to bear the grief of a baby you carried for only a short amount of time. I want you to know: losing your unborn baby is a grief worth grieving. A real, live, human has passed away. This is a gut-wrenching reality. No woman should feel shame over her need for others to help her bear this heavy burden.

A lot of women don't reach out for help because they know it will make them susceptible to painful comments about their baby. This is a valid fear. Wrong views of life in the womb have affected the way we speak about pre-born babies, even in Christian circles. Some people also just don't know what to say and often say the wrong thing without realizing it. However, sometimes we must risk hearing hurtful words to find the people who God has provided to walk with us in our grief. The benefits of Christian community outweigh the risks. We are all sinful; we all get hurt from time to time—but we still need each other.

## The Gift of the Church

Weary saint, God has given you the church to make it through the days and nights of pregnancy loss. The church may be full of sinners who make mistakes, but she is still the bride of Christ (Revelation 19:7). She is still a gift that he uses to provide for and comfort those suffering the loss of their baby. He is not finished with her—with *us*. We must uphold the church as the gift it is, even as we confront its need for growth.

We get to be a part of that growth. We can teach other Christians how to help women who are experiencing the loss of babies in the womb. As experiencing grief grows our compassion for others, we learn better how to comfort them. As believers, the hands and feet of Jesus, grow in compassion, the body shows itself to be an indispensable gift to every Christian—just as God intended.

## Prayer of Lament

I am weary with my moaning;
every night I flood my bed with tears;
I drench my couch with my weeping.
My eye wastes away because of grief;
it grows weak because of all my foes. (Psalm 6:6–7)

## Guided Lament

God, I am so weary of grief. I want my baby to be here. I want all of this to be undone. I weep every day for what could have been. Sustain my faith, God. For Jesus's sake. Amen.

## Bring Your Lament to God:

# Chapter 11

# The Gift of Compassion and Comfort toward Others

## *Lord, Bring Healing from My Grief*

*It wasn't the plant she brought,*
*or the soup she made.*
*Nor was it the words spoken,*
*or the Scripture shared.*
*Love was in the quiet tears that*
*gathered,*
*like soldiers,*
*ready to go to war,*
*holding me up in the battle.*

*Contractions gripped my abdomen* as I released the air from my lungs. Tingling sensations rippled through my entire body—

a feeling of cold numbness—like jumping into a lake of ice. Shades of black closed in on my mind as I crawled from the bathroom into the hallway. My husband rushed to me, scooping me into his lap. "Breathe with me. You're hyperventilating. You need to breathe." I writhed in his arms, doing my best to match my breathing to his. I was slick with sweat when the threat of unconsciousness had finally passed, along with my child. No one had prepared me for this. It was labor. Labor, *too soon*.

A couple days after losing our first baby, a woman from church asked to come over. She came bearing a plant and a heart to listen. She heard my fears and my questions, my sorrow and my confusion. I saw tears glisten along her lash lines as I spoke. When I finished, she thoughtfully shared her own story of miscarriage and stillbirth. She had also experienced labor too soon. In the course of just one visit, two acquaintances became linked together through Christ and shared grief. She didn't offer up explanations for why my baby died. No platitudes lingered in the air between us. She simply listened, wept with me, and shared in my sorrow. A burden-bearer, swooping in with the comfort of presence, the comfort of tears, and the comfort of Christ.

## The God of All Comfort

Many Christians can attest to the truth that we grow in compassion toward those who are suffering when we experience our own seasons of grief. It makes sense, considering what God's word says in 2 Corinthians 1:

> "Blessed be the God and Father of our Lord Jesus Christ, the Father of mercies and God of all comfort, who comforts us in all our affliction, so that we may be able to comfort those who are in any affliction, with the comfort with which we ourselves are comforted by God. For as we share abundantly in Christ's sufferings, so through Christ we share abundantly in comfort too." (vv. 3–5)

Our Savior is the Man of Sorrows, and our God is the God of all comfort. He comforts us in our afflictions so that we can comfort others in theirs. A friend of mine recently made the point that if sinful humans (including unbelievers) can empathize with others, albeit imperfectly, surely the God of the universe displays *perfect* empathy. In him is the flawless comfort all of us need, at the exact moment we need it. This comfort is ushered in by his presence with us both through his Spirit and through his people. If God is the God of all comfort, then we as his image bearers image him when we comfort others.

Isaiah 43 says,

> "Fear not, for I have redeemed you;
> I have called you by name, you are mine.
> When you pass through the waters, I will be with you;
> and through the rivers, they shall not overwhelm you;
> when you walk through fire you shall not be burned,
> and the flame shall not consume you.
> For I am the LORD your God,
> the Holy One of Israel, your Savior." (vv. 1b–3a)

Our Redeemer and Savior is with us through the rapid waters and raging fires of pregnancy loss. Even when it doesn't feel like it, we know the truth found in his word remains. His Spirit lives in us, keeping us afloat in the storm and holding the fire back from consuming our faith. When we walk through our darkest moments of loss to brighter days, we will look back and see how God sustained and refined our faith in him through it all, how he was holding us as we wrestled and as we wept.

In my greatest moments of loneliness, I see clearly that he was there, consoling me, leaving threads of evidence through his people that he was near. Having walked through miscarriage and experienced his comfort, I now long to comfort others with the comfort I received. It seems the way we grow in compassion for other sufferers is by walking through the fire of grief ourselves.

## Growing in Compassion

A few years before my husband and I began trying to grow our family, a friend of mine walked through a miscarriage. I was sad for her, but I didn't fully understand what she was going through. I shudder to think how my thoughts revealed a wrong view of children in the womb. I treated her suffering as more like the loss of a dream. But she didn't lose a dream; she was grieving a *life*. A baby who was alive—a precious soul who took up residence in her body. She felt the evidence of their life inside her and then she felt their death as they slipped from her womb and through her fingers. It wasn't until death reached into my own womb that I recognized my ignorance.

When we meet someone who lacks compassion for those who are suffering miscarriage (or any type of suffering), it is usually because they have suffered little, or they hold a stoical view of grief. It's easy to judge the grief of another when we have not experienced our own. Likewise, if we've been taught that sorrow is sinful, we will be harsh with those who are sorrowful.

But praise God! He is growing all of us in compassion toward those who are grieving. As we tread the waters of grief, the Holy Spirit grows our hearts in compassion for the grieving. We learn that every human handles grief differently. That each of us have different personalities, struggles, fears, family dynamics, support systems, and so on, that all contribute to our experience of grief. We recognize that platitudes usually only compound the hurt. We begin to give a suffering saint grace to question, cry, and wrestle with God. Their laments no longer make us uncomfortable but are seen as faith in God on display.

## Comforting Others

One of the most beautiful and life-giving parts of my life has been to come alongside women who are facing the grief of miscarriage. I grieve their loss, but rejoice in the God who has been kind enough to use me to comfort others through his comfort. Truly, it is a joy to spend ourselves, offering up our presence for the sake of comforting our sisters who have lost babies. Here are a few ways we can offer the comfort we have received from the God of all comfort:

*Listen to them.* Sometimes a woman needs someone to listen to her story, allowing her to wrestle through all the feelings of her loss. She wants to talk about her baby. She doesn't need answers to her questions. The loss of her baby isn't something that can be fixed.

*Offer our presence.* Other times, women may just need the physical presence of someone. A friend who is willing to sit alongside them in the weighty silence of grief. They don't want to talk about it; but they also don't want to be alone.

*Pray with them.* When in doubt, pray. Offer prayers to God for comfort, rest, and physical healing. Send prayers through text, email, or a letter.

*Lament with them.* This goes along with prayer but is a specific way we can encourage our sisters as they grieve their baby. We can lament to God on their behalf over the loss of this precious life. When they feel too weak to pray, we can bring their questions to our Father for them. This is one way we bear their burden.

*Depend on the Holy Spirit to guide any encouragement.* Walking with others through grief can be tricky. It's hard to know when to speak, share Scripture, or offer truths about God. Should we confront wrong thinking? Should we call out sin in the midst of their tears? There is so much that could be said about this, but the thing we must remember is this: the Holy Spirit is our guide. We must pray throughout our entire time with a sister, seeking wisdom from above. He will show us when to speak and when to remain quiet, when to share a passage of Scripture and when to close our lips. God promises to give us words and wisdom when we need it, if only we would ask (James 1:5).

*Provide for their physical needs.* We know how hard it can be both physically and mentally just to make it through each day of grief. We can provide meals, transportation, our presence at appointments, care packages, and childcare. We can buy groceries, clean their home, pack up the nursery, mow their grass, and tend to their garden. There are many ways we can support them by providing physical help.

*Check on them often.* As time passes, people forget and isolation can set in. It's so comforting when friends and family show they care by asking how we are doing and acknowledging that it's okay that we are still sad over our baby.

*Remember their baby with them.* Dates like Mother's Day, due dates, and anniversaries are painful for women who have lost their baby. We can show we love them by remembering their baby too. Acknowledging their grief on these specific days validates the life of their child.

*When in doubt, ask.* Sometimes it's hard to know what a friend needs when she has lost a baby. To avoid overwhelming her with simply asking what she needs, it's helpful to give her options from which she can choose. "I'm bringing you food. Would you rather me leave it at your door or come in for a bit to help around the house?" To give another example: "If you're available, I'd like to come over. I can either bring a movie or we can talk. I'm here for you." Sometimes it's hard to ask for help. Questions like this take the pressure off by giving a choice.

What would you add? I'm sure there are many other ways we can comfort our sisters as they walk through miscarriage.

## The Gift of Pointing to the God of All Comfort

In the midst of my third loss, a mentor drove nearly forty minutes to my house and then drove me to my appointment so I didn't have to go alone. She sat with me in the exam room; her presence was like a warm blanket while you're sick. She provided for and comforted me in my time of need. I want to be that person for others now.

Ultimately, when we travel the tragic terrain of losing a baby, we are given the gift of growing in compassion and comfort toward others. We take comfort in our God who is the God of all comfort, and we display his goodness through comforting the hurting. We are the hands and feet of Jesus, created for good works that glorify him and build up the body (Ephesians 2:10). When we weep with those who weep, we are walking in those very works.

We get the honor of being Jesus to those who are grieving, pointing them to the true source of comfort: his ultimate love. His steadfast love that never lets go. And in this—in *him*—we, too, find great comfort in the face of miscarriage.

## Psalm of Lament

Save me, O God!
    For the waters have come up to my neck.
I sink in deep mire,
    where there is no foothold;
I have come into deep waters,
    and the flood sweeps over me.
I am weary with my crying out;
    my throat is parched.
My eyes grow dim
    with waiting for my God. (Psalm 69:1–3)

## Guided Lament

Lord, I feel like I'm drowning in the pain of loss. I've been crying out to you for so long and yet I'm still waiting for you to help me. It feels like the storm will never end. Amen.

## Bring Your Lament to God:

## Chapter 12

# The Gift of Deeper Intimacy with Christ

### *Lord, You Are the Treasure above All Treasures*

*Turn your eyes upon Jesus,*
*Look full in His wonderful face,*
*And the things of earth will grow strangely dim,*
*In the light of His glory and grace.*
—"Turn Your Eyes Upon Jesus" by Helen Howarth Lemmel

*I sat in a blue beach chair*, feet buried in the sand. The sun that morning glared through an overcast sky as I watched my husband wade in the ocean. Setting my book on my lap, I peered into the deep blue before me when a woman, round with a baby, strolled into my view as she followed her toddler. Melancholy fell around me like a light summer rain. My throat tightened, but tears failed to follow. Sadness wedged itself in my throat, making it hard to breathe. It felt like a century passed before I could swallow down the sorrow. Behold, the sign of familiar pain—the kind that lingers in the background like a pilot light. This is one symptom of a heart that longs, a heart that is sick with grief, a heart where waiting feels endless. We were on our much-anticipated anniversary trip that August, fresh on the heels of losing our third baby just two months before. It was supposed to be a reprieve from all the pain we had lived through that year. For me, it was running away from weariness. But grief found me there.

I watched as the woman with the long dark hair played in the sand with her son and husband. I wondered what it would be like to build sandcastles and show my babies the way God makes waves crash upon the shore. I looked at the heaviness of her womb and thought, *How right and good. Babies should live. Bellies should grow.* My hand rested on my own stomach where three babies once were, where a baby should have been. I wasn't envious; I had grown to rejoice over each new life that flourished. No, I wasn't jealous, I was *grieved*. And I desperately missed my babies.

## Who or What Do We Treasure?

Not long before our first baby passed, our pastor at the time was preaching through Philippians. Paul's complete surrender to and love for the Lord left me in awe. He says, "But whatever gain I had, I counted as loss for the sake of Christ. Indeed, I count everything as loss because of the surpassing worth of knowing Christ Jesus my

Lord" (Philippians 3:7–8a). I wondered, "What would it be like to truly value Christ as most precious? How would it change my life to treasure him above all things?" I wrote on the top of the page in my Bible, "Value Christ above all," and prayed, "Lord, help me to treasure you more."

I'll never forget the shame that flooded my body and made my heart race when an acquaintance told me, "Once you stop idolizing a baby, God will give you one." A woman who barely knew me had made a severe judgment: God's withholding equals my sin. She claimed I had traded my Savior for a baby—that I was clinging to the gift rather than the Giver. I looked in my heart and found her to be a liar. I loved my babies, but I truly loved God more. Unfortunately, when a woman loses babies or battles infertility, it is often assumed she must be discontent in Christ. If she were content, then God would give her a baby. This is not true. A gift withheld does not equal an idol we hold. Our lack is not evidence of faithlessness. Our empty arms are not a result of unrepentant sin.

And yet, God can use our grief to draw us nearer to himself, causing us to grow in contentment, because in his presence is fullness of joy and complete satisfaction (Psalm 16:11). It seems that, for the sake of our own joy, it may be a valid question to ask ourselves, who or what do we most treasure? If it is not Christ, how can we grow toward making him the treasure of our hearts? For we know Jesus himself said, "For where your treasure is, there your heart will be also" (Matthew 6:21).

## Envy or Grief?

When a woman walks through a season of miscarriage or infertility, she will be met with hoards of soul-pricking reminders. Due dates, pregnancy announcements, baby showers, or a stranger's swollen abdomen can leave her reeling with feelings of grief, envy, or both. Sometimes we don't know exactly what we're feeling; we just know it *hurts*. Our hearts are breaking, and life without our baby is so painful.

Some Christians view any kind of sadness as a sign that a person is not finding their hope in Christ. To believe so would be to expect more from our fellow humans than their Creator does. Contentment is not the absence of sadness, but rather to be resolved in our belief that Jesus is enough, no matter our circumstances.

After the birth of my second son, I couldn't walk for weeks from severe SI joint dysfunction and sciatica in my leg. Physical therapy, a steroid, a walker, and time helped me heal enough to where I could get around. I was feeling a bit more like myself when I jumped through the sprinkler with my oldest son. Immediately, searing nerve pain was revived. I had almost forgotten about my injury only to be violently awakened to the pain. Similarly, pregnancy announcements can come as a shock to a woman who has recently experienced a miscarriage. She was learning to live with her grief in the background. These reminders can bring it forward.

It might be easy for onlookers to misjudge the state of her heart as envious. They forget that right after Scripture calls us to rejoice with those who rejoice, it also says to weep with those who weep. This means we do both simultaneously. We rejoice with women in the gift of new life, and at the same time, we weep with women over the loss of their baby. Surely, the woman walking through loss should be given grace to grieve even as she rejoices with the woman who has received a baby. We cannot lock up our sorrow in a tidy little box in the attic of our minds, only taking it out when it is convenient. It is normal that life's reminders will cause us to shed fresh tears. Experiencing the rekindling of grief over losing our baby at the sight of these reminders is not the same as envy.

What do we do when our grief is brought to the surface by a baby shower or a pregnancy announcement? Do we stuff our feelings down and try to ignore them? Do we heap shame on ourselves for missing our baby? No. We must address our grief with God. Depending on the circumstances, that might mean logging off social media and bringing our grief to the feet of our Father through prayers of lament. At a gathering, it may look like taking a moment to go to the bathroom and praying for the Spirit's help in rejoicing with our sister as we grieve. It may mean we have to forgo baby showers for a time. Depending on the relationship, sometimes this might look like two friends—one who is pregnant and the other who is pregnant with loss—rejoicing, weeping, and praying together.

Sometimes we feel a mixture of grief and envy. It's important that we don't deny ourselves permission to grieve our precious baby while also seeking to put away any envy in our heart. Longing for our baby, feeling the sadness of life without them, thinking about the would be's ("My baby would be the same age as hers." "I would be 20 weeks pregnant today."), wondering how it would feel to hold them—these are thoughts and feelings of grief, not envy or discontentment.

Envy holds in it a state of entitlement. Envy says, "I deserve a baby because I _______."

... would be a better mother than her.

... love God and she doesn't.

... have experienced more suffering than her and deserve a break.

... have been waiting longer than her.

... was hurt by her.

When we are consumed with thoughts that display why *we* deserve a baby more than someone else, we know we have crossed from the safe waters of grief to the rapid currents of envy. And envy, when left unchecked, will only lead us off a cliff, falling fast down a waterfall of harm—harm to ourselves and harm to others.

## Envying Our Sister

My closest friend and I both had a rough entrance into motherhood. While my husband and I walked through loss after loss, she and her husband struggled to conceive. The day she came to church and shared with me the amazing news that she was pregnant, I genuinely cried tears of joy for her. I was so thankful and hopeful that her journey of infertility was coming to a close.

The next morning, I held a pregnancy test in my hand and examined it closely. I held it up toward the bright bathroom light fixture. No line. *Maybe this bathroom is too dark*, I thought to myself. I quickly walked to the back door where the sunlight shone in. I peered at it again. Squinting and blinking and bargaining, I fought hard to see two lines on that little white test. *Could there be a faint line? Oh Lord, please let there be a faint line.* There wasn't. It was negative. No baby had taken root in my womb, and those supposed symptoms I'd been feeling proved to be simply taunting me, giving me false hope that life had begun to flourish where I'd only seen it die.

My journey of loss and infertility continued for many more months. Before my friend had her first baby, I lost my third. I held many babies during that season, but none of them were mine. My husband and I took our place as the only young couple in our church who had no living children. I distinctly remember one Sunday standing in a corner of the foyer as I watched my friends chatting in a circle, a baby in the arms of each one. The temptation toward envious thoughts surrounded me in that season, and bitterness hung around like the squirrels that hang on my bird feeder.

How do we fight against this temptation to compare our lot to our sisters in Christ whose babies are still alive? It's helpful to go back to the basics. We must remember the *imago Dei.* God has created every single baby, whether born in heaven or on earth, to image him to the world. Each human conceived has innate value, worth, and purpose, no matter the number of their days. With this truth in mind, we can separate the baby in our friend's belly or arms from the loss of our own baby. We can know their child is not a sleight of God's hand toward us. It doesn't mean our friend, family member, or even our enemy is more loved by God. God has a purpose for every child, and it is to bring him glory.

Scripture calls us to rejoice with our sister (Romans 12:15). This includes when they receive what we've lost. This doesn't mean that we can't also experience our own grief as we do so. We can praise God for his gift to our sister while also weeping over the loss of our own. Feeling sorrow over our baby is not the same as refusing to rejoice with our sister. By God's power, joy and sorrow can intertwine. The problem comes when we refuse to rejoice with another by avoiding them, feeling resentful toward them or God, or wishing harm upon them or their baby.

## Envying Unbelievers

While the above truths still apply to addressing envy in our hearts toward unbelievers, there's a tragic difference we must consider. In Psalm 73, Asaph lays out his honest feelings to which many of us can relate. He says, "For I was envious of the arrogant when I saw the prosperity of the wicked. For they have no pangs until death; their bodies are fat and sleek. They are not in trouble as others are; they are not stricken like the rest of mankind" (vv. 3–5).

Have you ever felt this way? A woman has a one-night stand and ends up pregnant, then tragically has an abortion. Another woman gets pregnant and continues to do illicit drugs during her entire pregnancy, leaving her child to suffer the consequences of withdrawal once born. Meanwhile, we lost our babies. These are harsh realities that anger us. And they should. We should be angered by the harm done to children. It's natural to ask God why we lost the baby we wanted when women across the world willingly have theirs stripped from their womb every day.

When our atheist cousin becomes pregnant after we just lost our baby, we might find ourselves wondering why her and not us? We love God. Why did he give a baby to someone who hates him? Asaph wondered something similar: "All in vain have I kept my heart clean and washed my hands in innocence. For all the day long I have been stricken and rebuked every morning" (73:13–14).

"God, I have served you and loved you for years. My husband and I were faithful to your word, saving sex for marriage. We would teach our child about you and disciple them in your word. Why did you give a baby to a non-believer when ours died?"

Have you had similar questions? I know I did while walking through my miscarriages. Why does God bless unbelievers with gifts his children desire? This question hijacks our minds, tempting our hearts to grow resentful toward God and ignorant to the truth of his goodness toward us (vv. 21–22).

But look at what Asaph finds when he goes to God with this question: "But when I thought how to understand this, it seemed to me a wearisome task, until I went into the sanctuary of God; *then I discerned their end*" (vv. 16–17, *emphasis added*). What is the end of those who do not repent and turn to Jesus Christ alone to save them from their sin? They will perish. They will bear the wrath of God on their backs for all eternity. David speaks to this in Psalm 37 when he warns, "Fret not yourself because of evildoers; be not envious of wrongdoers!" (v. 1). Why? Because they will fade and wither like grass (v. 2).

This is not something we should rejoice in. Instead of envying the earthly gift of a child, this truth should lead us to be overcome with compassion for the lost and filled with gratitude to God for the gift of eternal life through Christ. It should renew our compassion and desire to seek the lost; it should reorient our minds to view the Giver as better than the gift.

Because of our salvation in Christ, which can never be taken from us, we can join the psalmist and say even in our grief, "The lines have fallen for me in pleasant places; indeed, I have a beautiful inheritance" (Psalm 16:6). The wombs of unbelievers, whose portion is in this life only, may be filled with treasure, but the people of God receive the true Treasure—the Treasure above all treasures: *Jesus* (Psalm 17:14–15). Our portion is Jesus. *We* have the good portion.

## Jesus is the True Treasure

We who have felt the ache of loss touch our wombs, taking with it one of the most treasured gifts of our life, know a deep grief. Our arms and hearts feel the emptiness caused by the loss of our precious baby. Still, there is a treasure that can never be stolen from us. His name is Jesus, the one who has borne all our grief, the true Treasure.

Grief has a way of drawing us to him, the only one who can truly understand our pain. Yet sometimes it feels like it is doing the opposite. We might experience feelings of anger toward God or fears of abandonment. Maybe instead of drawing near to God, we find ourselves running away from him. We might even be tempted to walk away from the faith altogether. Yet it may be during these very seasons in our life when we feel him hold onto us with the grip of his steadfast love, strengthening our faith even when we can't see it.

One of the lowest points throughout my losses was when I felt utterly abandoned by God. I was weeping and praying on the couch in our living room yet sensed no comfort in return. In past sorrows, I had been keenly aware of his presence with me, but in this moment, I felt completely alone. It is only by the power of the Holy Spirit who held onto me when I could no longer cling to Christ that my faith survived. Now, those moments are treasured memories of God's sustaining grace in my life. You and I can take comfort in Psalm 73:26 which says, "My flesh and my heart may fail, but God is the strength of my heart and my portion forever." When our hearts fail us, God still holds us. He's been holding us all along.

God longs for you and me to behold his goodness that brings joy through the weeping. In your grief, you can receive more of the comforting presence of Jesus. You can know your suffering Savior, the Man of Sorrows. To know him more is to treasure him more. Jesus is not a consolation prize for the loss of your unborn baby; he *is* the prize—the Treasure that surpasses all other treasures. In his presence there is fullness of joy and pleasures forevermore (Psalm 16:11).

Jesus is the Treasure who hung upon a cross for you and me. He's the Son of God who never sinned, yet became sin that "in him we might become the righteousness of God" (2 Corinthians 5:21). His sacrifice eradicated all our sin, and then he gave us his perfectly obedient life as if we had lived it ourselves. He's the God who elected, called, and justified us. He is working even now as you read to sanctify you, and he will bring us all safely into glory one day. What *grace*. Hallelujah, what a Savior! What a *Treasure*.

My miscarriages were not good, but God is good. I saw his goodness in the midst of immense suffering. He uses all things in our life, both good and bad, to draw us to himself. My losses were no different. As my heart desired a baby—not just a baby but *my* babies—I was given opportunities to experience a deeper intimacy with Christ. Laid before me was a choice: turn away from the Lord and harden my heart or run to him with all its shattered pieces. I could try to pull myself up by my own self-sufficient bootstraps or I could take refuge in the Great Comforter, my Strong Tower. One would lead me away from him; the other would bring about true comfort and communion with God.

The truth is, I could not bear up under the storm of pregnancy loss without the strength of God sustaining my faith. As I ran to him with my lament and sorrow, I experienced his perfect care for me. His tender mercy and grace left me with no choice but to love him more. In my losses, though the emptiness of my womb felt like a black hole that would swallow me, I experienced the nearness of my Lord. My heart began to treasure Christ more. God had answered my prayer.

## The Treasure Will Bring Us Home

I have never longed for heaven more than I do now after losing my babies. I miss them and long to be with them. More than that, I long to be near to Christ. Sometimes I catch myself, eyes fixed on the clouds, imagining what it will be like to see Jesus in them, descending to take me home. At the trumpet sound, when we're caught up in the clouds with him, will our faces shine with his glory? Will the warmth of his smile feel like sunshine on our cheeks? After the final war is won and we stand in the new heavens and new earth, will it feel like a never-ending, beautiful, spring day? Will the trees burst forth with white petals and tulips cover every field? Will bunnies frolic all around us and birds sing a hymn of praise to the Creator? Words utterly fail me; can we even fathom what he has in store for us?

Like the feeling you get on that first warm day after a long winter, one day the winter of this life and all the grief it holds in it will *flee*. New life—life eternal—will spring up all around us at the coming of our Savior. He will usher in perfect joy and wipe away every tear we've ever cried. And we will be home.

I know you are hurting. I know that the grief of your baby is hard to bear. You aren't meant to bear it alone. Jesus is drawing near to you in your suffering. He will sustain your faith. He is weeping with you, grieving your baby. And he offers himself to you, today, right now. In his hands is a deeper intimacy with him that is yours for the taking. Take hold of him. Cling to him like the Treasure he is—the Treasure who gave up his life to save you. He can never be stolen from you. He is the Treasure above all treasures. And when you feel your arms are too weak to cling to him, the True Treasure will never lose his grip on you.

## Psalm of Lament

Out of the depths I cry to you, O LORD!
O Lord, hear my voice!
Let your ears be attentive
to the voice of my pleas for mercy!

If you, O LORD, should mark iniquities,
O Lord, who could stand?
But with you there is forgiveness,
that you may be feared.

I wait for the LORD, my soul waits,
and in his word I hope;
my soul waits for the Lord
more than watchmen for the morning,
more than watchmen for the morning. (Psalm 130:1–6)

## Guided Lament

Father, I have nothing else I can do but wait for you. Wait for healing, for peace, for a child, for rest. Please draw near to me. Please show me your faithfulness. For Jesus's sake. Amen.

## Bring Your Lament to God:

# A Note to Pastors and Church Leaders

*I praise God* for pastors and church leaders like you who want to better support those in your congregation suffering miscarriage. As a shepherd, much of the need for growth in how the church can support men and women experiencing pregnancy loss falls on your shoulders. It is a heavy weight, yet one God has entrusted to you. I hope that this book will be a practical and helpful resource for you.

As you navigate these troubled waters, here are eight things to never lose sight of when coming alongside couples in your congregation who are suffering from miscarriage:

*They lost more than a pregnancy.* They lost a baby—an image-bearer of God whom they loved. Allow them to grieve this family member. If it is a practice of your church to send out an email informing the congregation when a member has lost a loved one, then this should be done for couples who lose babies in the womb, too (with permission).

*Cover their grief with grace.* The grief of your congregants is fragile and should be handled thoughtfully. Beware of expecting more from a grieving couple than the Bible expects of them. Do not judge their tears. If they say something you believe to be unbiblical, don't rush in to correct them, but instead understand that grief is raw and allow them to wrestle, question, and grieve their baby for as long as they need. Come alongside them in prayer and with a listening ear as they work through their grief..

*Practice lamenting as a church.* Often missing from prayer meetings and worship services is a time of corporate lament. As believers we have much to rejoice in, but we still live in a broken world. There may be opportunities to lament that are naturally available to us in our services if we have eyes to see. Maybe it's a psalm or a time of prayer for those who are hurting. Practicing lament as a church bonds a local body as they bear each other's burdens and losses together. We are weeping *with those who weep.* This creates a safe environment for members of the church to grieve openly.

*Keep reaching out.* The scars of miscarriage are long-lasting for many couples. Reminders of loss hide around every bend. Sometimes couples experience recurrent loss or infertility after loss, meaning they suffer for many years after the initial miscarriage. Leaders should schedule visits to their house to pray with them, not just in the beginning, but even months later. Consider recording the death date and telling them you're praying for them on the anniversary of their loss.

*Be extra sensitive on holidays.* Holidays like Mother's Day and Father's Day can be especially painful for couples who have no living children. Church leaders should acknowledge moms and dads who have lost babies as well as those who are battling infertility. Consider the suffering of these congregants as you plan services on these days.

*Pray for them publicly.* If a time of pastoral prayer is a practice in your church service, pray a general prayer for couples walking through miscarriage from time to time. You can also pray for couples by name if they feel comfortable with this.

*Connect them with others who have experienced similar loss.* If you know of a woman who has experienced miscarriage, ask her if she would be willing to come alongside other women in your church who are grieving similar losses.

*Check on fathers.* They are often overlooked in the grief of miscarriage, but husbands need support too. If you see them at church, ask how they're doing or if they need anything. Don't assume they aren't hurting.

The loss of a baby in the womb is a painful, often misunderstood grief. May God go before you, giving you wisdom, grace, and love as you walk alongside the men and women in your church who are suffering this loss.

> For this God is our God for ever and ever;
>     he will be our guide even to the end. (Psalm 48:14 NIV)

# Notes

1 Mary Carey, "Upon Ye Sight of My Abortive Birth Ye 31th: Of December 1657," *Poetry Explorer*, https://www.poetryexplorer.net/poem.php?id=10046105.

2 Eve Keller, "Embryonic Individuals: The Rhetoric of Seventeenth-Century Embryology and the Construction of Early-Modern Identity," *Eighteenth-Century Studies* 33, no. 3 (2000): 321–48, https://doi.org/10.1353/ecs.2000.0027. Quote from page 327.

3 Mary Bushnell Cheney to Frank Cheney, July 9, 1879. Shannon Withycombe, "Happy Miscarriages: An Emotional History of Pregnancy Loss," Nursing Clio, November 12, 2015, https://nursingclio.org/2015/11/12/happy-miscarriages-an-emotional-history-of-pregnancy-loss/.

4 Diary entry of Maria Heyde, November 15 ,1862. Quoted in Felicity Jensz, "Miscarriage and Coping in the Mid-Nineteenth Century: Private Notes from Distant Places," *Gender & History* 32, no. 2 (April 29, 2020): 270–85, https://doi.org/10.1111/1468-0424.12478.

5 Abraham Verghese, "Where Do Babies Come from? And Why Did It Take Scientists so Long to Find Out?," *The New York*

*Times*, June 23, 2017, https://www.nytimes.com/2017/06/23/books/review/the-seeds-of-life-edward-dolnick.html.

6 "The Thin Blue Line: The History of the Pregnancy Test," National Institutes of Health, https://history.nih.gov/display/history/Pregnancy+Test+Timeline.

7 Steven Andrew Jacobs, "The Scientific Consensus on When a Human's Life Begins," *Issues in Law and Medicine* (Fall 2021): 221–33, https://pubmed.ncbi.nlm.nih.gov/36629778/.

8 Li Cohen, "Michelle Williams Advocates for Abortion Rights in Golden Globes Acceptance Speech," CBS News, January 6, 2020, https://www.cbsnews.com/news/golden-globes-michelle-williams-advocates-for-womens-rights-in-golden-globes-speech/.

9 Nancy Pearcey, *Love Thy Body: Answering Hard Questions about Life and Sexuality* (Grand Rapids: Baker, 2019), 50.

10 Pearcey, *Love Thy Body*, 51–52.

11 Psalm 56:8a.

12 Mark Vroegop, *Dark Clouds, Deep Mercy: Discovering the Grace of Lament* (Wheaton, IL: Crossway, 2019), 28.

13 John Calvin, Aaron C. Denlinger, and Burk Parsons, *A Little Book on the Christian Life* (Orlando, FL: Reformation Trust Publishing, 2017), 78.

14 Kelly M. Kapic, *Embodied Hope: A Theological Meditation on Pain and Suffering* (Downers Grove, IL: IVP Academic, 2017), 47.

15 Esther Fleece, *No More Faking Fine: Ending the Pretending* (Grand Rapids: Zondervan, 2017), 43.

16 Vroegop, *Dark Clouds, Deep Mercy*, 21.

17 Jennifer Greenburg, (@JennMGreenberg),"I don't care how Reformed or Five Pointed you think you are, if you think depression or anxiety are sins your theology is Prosperity Gospel backwash." Twitter, January 17, 2023, 9:18 p.m., https://twitter.com/JennMGreenberg/status/1615534055499374593.

18 Corrie Ten Boom, Elizabeth Sherrill, and John Sherill, *The Hiding Place* (Grand Rapids: Chosen Books, 2006), 210.

19 Grant Macaskill, "The Spirit & the Presence of Christ: Crying 'Abba' in the Ruins of War," I No Longer Live, but Christ Lives in Me: The Reformed Self in Paul (lecture, Orlando, FL, 2018), https://rts.edu/resources/the-spirit-the-presence-of-christ-crying-abba-in-the-ruins-of-war/.

20 "Recurrent Pregnancy Loss," *Yale Medicine*, February 10, 2023, https://www.yalemedicine.org/conditions/recurrent-pregnancy-loss.

21 Mayo Clinic Staff, "Pregnancy after Miscarriage: What you need to know," Mayo Clinic, October 27, 2021, https://www.mayoclinic.org/healthy-lifestyle/getting-pregnant/in-depth/pregnancy-after-miscarriage/art-20044134.

22 "Amos – Baby Name Meaning, Origin, and Popularity," Nameberry, March 2023, https://nameberry.com/babyname/amos/boy.

23 Chris Tomlin, "All the Way My Savior Leads Me," *Genius*, https://genius.com/Chris-tomlin-all-the-way-my-savior-leads-me-lyrics.

24 Rachel Joy Welcher, *Sometimes Women Lie About Being Okay: Poems and Sketches* (Vermillion, SD: Dustlings Press, 2022), 71–72.

25 "What is the Benefit of a Word Fitly Spoken? (Proverbs 25:11)," Got Questions, https://www.gotquestions.org/word-fitly-spoken.html.